In loving memory of

Willie and Onnie King
Rosetta Robinson
Andre, Demetrius, Wilber, Daniel and Nikita Tillman

ACKNOWLEDGEMENTS

I would not be who I am and where I am without my Lord and savior Jesus Christ and the gifts he's given me. Without Him I'm nothing. Not only has he blessed and entrusted me with these gifts, but he placed into my life the people, things and experiences that helped form and guide my creativity. It goes without saying that I am forever indebted to Him. I pray that one day I will hear you say, well done thou good and faithful servant.

Bishop Horace E. Smith (Apostolic Faith Church), my pastor. Thank you for your spiritual teachings and guidance and for the Godly examples you continue to show not only in your words, but in your deeds. You've shown me how to walk with honor and integrity and because of this I am a better husband, father and man. I pray God continues to bless you and your family for your commitment to Him.

Jonathan and Jacinta Banks, not only for your wise counsel that you've given me over the years, but because of your sacrifice to me and my family, you've allowed us to have a dream come true while putting dreams of your own on hold. Words cannot fully express the love my family and I have for you and we are committed through our actions to be a blessing to you and your family.

Troy Lewis, you are my friend and my brother. Your generosity has not gone unnoticed. Thanks for your continued support of me. Love ya man.

Reginald Bailey, it doesn't matter how long or how far we are from one and another we seem to never miss a beat when we connect. That's what's up. You're one of the few good friends in my life.

Warren and Royal Farley, thank you for being REAL. You're good people and when God truly gets ahold of you...devil watch out! Love you guys.

Sister Toni McCloud, your energy, your passion and love for what you do is inspiring. Thank you for being my Network teacher and putting me on the path that I'm on today.

Brother James Thomas, my friend and mentor. I thank God for our connection and for putting you in my life and showing me humility.

Minister Tim Brown, thanks for giving me good sound Godly advice and letting me know that God know my heart and my intentions. I'll continue to keep Him first in all that I do.

John Hughes (R.I.P), Spike Lee, Quentin Tarentino. It is because of their creativity, I'm able to freely express myself through words, trusting my instincts and my own voice and vision. I dare to be uniquely different. I dare to be me.

To all of the poets in and around Chicago I simply say thanks for your inspiration... peace & love.

TO MY FAMILY

My daughter and first born child Ayesha, you have beauty and intelligence and were fearfully and wonderfully made and I am very proud of. You keep me up to date on my wardrobe and style and share my same sense of humor; you're so much like your mom. I know you're going to make an impact in this world.

To my first son Kevin Jr. who carries my name, you've always had a special place in my heart. There is crazy potential in you, son. God is going to use you to do great things.

For Quentin my youngest, sky's the limits for you. You're strong and gifted in so many ways. You are a born leader. Keep moving in the right direction with patience.

To the love of my life and a true help mate my wife, Barbara. There's so much I appreciate about you, things that I couldn't see at the beginning but, have since had the privilege to know and understand. It was you who gave me the stage name, Kharacter, because you said you saw many side of me as a performer and that the name just fit. You were right. You are my greatest supporter and critic who continues to encourage and motivate me. You've been by my side through the good and bad times and you continue to be the rock for our family. There's so much that I owe you. You are the driving force behind this book as you would always tell me, stop talking about it and do it and this is the result. Because of you I push myself and will continue to do so. The word of God says; whoso findeth a wife findeth a good thing and obtaineth favor of the Lord (Proverbs 18:22). No truer scripture resonates more for me about you than this. Eighteen years of marriage and twenty plus years of knowing you and we're still, yet holding on. I love you, baby. I truly do, 10/10/09.

Chapter 1

<u>DISCOVERY</u>

Poetry and I in the beginning

MY FIRST POEM...simple and true

JUDGEMENT
Written by
Kevin K. King Sr.

Everyone must face you and account for how we lived
Did we live for you the holy way the life you chose to give?

Did we honor your name for all it's worth and fear you above all else
Or had we simply obliged in indulging in things to satisfy ourselves

From the smallest of deeds that have been done by everyone you know
You'll call our name and up we'll stand and down the list you'll go

You have everything well documented from once we understood
What was right from what was wrong to knowing bad from good?

The choices we made to go against what we know we should not do
Are all adding up determining what gates we are to pass through

Now, the question is which one is more, which values have you kept
If not the good he guarantees the wages of sin is death

YOU NEVER KNOW WHO YOU'LL RUN INTO...

Have you ever told someone a lie to keep from doing something or going somewhere? This is poetic telling of such a story. There's an expression that goes be careful how you treat people because, you could be entertaining an angel. To that I would also like to add, you never know who God is sending your way and why.

YOU AGAIN
Written by
Kevin K. King Sr.
(KHARACTER)

I was asked one day if I'd like to attend this church service...
I was asked by this gentlemen
My response to this was a hefty excuse
And at no time at all did I cut myself loose
Now, as he went one way and I went another
I thought church on a Monday, not for this brother
I had nothing to do that day at all
But, church on a Monday, why that's Monday Night Football
Well, on the following day around the following time
I saw the same man but, I paid him no mind
We extended our hands to exchange pleasantries
Then he mentioned church services again that evening
Blindsided once more by this question again
My response...I'd be busy going to see a sick friend
As Wednesday arrived fourth day of the week
I avoided the usual time we would meet
Instead, I'd be ten minutes more late
But, when I arrived there he was with a smile on his face
My man, he said how does tonight look?
My man, I said as my head shook
Not good brother, not good at all...
In fact Thursday is looking to bad to call
But, optimistically sounding he said we'll see
So, come Thursday I decided even later I'll be
And I was as it came by thirty minutes more
But, when I arrived there he was same place same smile as before
Hey! Hey! He greeted me, same cheerful tone
Man, I thought I missed you he said

Yeah, man I thought you'd be gone
But, quick on my feet and before he could ask
I informed him of a previous engagement I had
He expressed sympathies that I couldn't attend
Then suggested maybe Friday I'd be able to join in
Well, maybe perhaps come Friday I could
And maybe perhaps come Friday I would
Anything could happen from one day to the next
But, the chances of me coming are a bit of a stretch
So, now it's Friday the day the fun begins
Anxiously anticipating the arrival of the weekend
Furthest thought on mind is dealing with this man
And the mentions of this church he hopes I'd attend
Now, this time as I cheerfully walked down the way
I was a lot more excited because it was payday
See, I had done a lot of overtime the previous weeks
So, I couldn't wait to receive the extra benefits I'd reap
Now, I'm walking down the street with that thought in mind
So, I never really heard this voice from behind
Instead, I find myself being pushed to the ground
As hails of bullets are being spread all around
And laying right there next to me during this
Is the same gentlemen I always tried to miss
Soon the sounds all around us came to a cease
As tires from a car pulled off to a screech
Said the gentlemen to me as he smiled through his teeth as we stood to
our feet dust ourselves to look neat
Are you alright? He asked me this, calm as can be
I don't know I said let me see
So, I checked for holes and traces of red
With the exception of a rather large knot on my head
Outside of that everything was okay
There was no ambulance needed to take me away

So, I turned to this man who just saved my life
Who risked his own fate to make sure I was alright
This man who jumped head first into danger
To save someone like me... a stranger
I turned to this man now being filled with delight and I asked him
What time are church services being held tonight?

COLOR BLIND...thanks for your assistance

PEN PAL
Written by
Kevin K. King Sr.
(Kharacter)

The weapon of choice I choose to declare is my writing
pen
So faithful and fair
Whether it's blue or black ink I don't care
For they are both quite eloquent to compare
With its fine tip point where ink thus comes out
Pressed down to paper which lies about
With it I write my inner most thoughts
Such fondness has my pen brought
As I gently hold you close
And move you about with such gentle strokes
With you I can write most anything
A poem or play of lyrics to sing
Perhaps a script of such noble taste
Full of colorful characters I'll create
A sincere letter to give to you
One of a secrete rondavu
I escape with you and travel far
My destination is to reach the heart
To spark a thought within the mind

In search of truth often hard to find
And when you've depleted all you ink
When you substance has become extinct
I momentarily pause to think
Reflecting on our common link
An overview of what we've done
The writer's block we've overcome
The excitement to finally reach that peak
The ending that we've come to reach
But, I'll trade not one moment of our time shared
When pulling all-nighters you were right there
So, this one poem I dedicate to you... my pen
No matter the color, anyone will do

THIS COULD BE ANYONE...A confession

Written by
Kevin K. King Sr.
(KHARACTER)

She was sixteen but, you couldn't tell
Fact was she carried herself as mature quite well
She never spoke in any way to indicate she was a teen
She didn't have to, assumed she was older than it
seemed

She didn't dress like a young girl however young girls
dress
She only dressed appropriate as one would expect
She never tried to pretend to be old enough
She simply looked the part of eighteen and up

She looked that way not just because of her face
See, she had developed at a most unusual pace
She at no time tried to conceal her age...it never entered
her mind
She was innocent in that way

She believed the compliments she was being told
She believed them as words that she could hold

She believed such words would never stear her wrong
She, in essence, had no idea of what was going on

She didn't know that these were lies being told to her
She wasn't asked if it were the truth she'd much prefer
She wasn't given a choice in the matter at all
She was deceived from the moment of that first call

She was just a young girl, she didn't know everything
She only knew who she was and that she was sixteen
She found out though but, by then it was too late
She had been used sexually abused...it was statutory
rape
She had her day though, that's when she pointed to me
Confession...from prisoner number 22173

Copyright August 13, 2002
Revised March 5, 2012

KNOW WHEN TO SAY WHEN...

A PUBLIC SERVICE ANNOUNCEMENT
Written by
Kevin K. King Sr.
(KHARACTER)

Hit the shop for the fade, other spot I cops the gear
I'm drinking Hennie straight up, no chaser no beer
See, we kicks it that night, just me and the crew
On a mission to position some honeys to do
Pockets sit swollen as if they've been workin' out
Spit the flow so they'll know what a players about
Watch the dimes gather around, they wanna sit with a star
So, they pop a spot next to me at the bar
They wanna know what's my name? What's my game? Who I be?
They wanna lay claim to other dames that they leavin' with me
Confidence steady risin' with every shot of the Hen
Top one off git the bar tender to hit me again
Liquor's got me trippin', still I continue to sip
Hit the curb tell the valet to bring me my whip
I got a honey on my arm and more willing to come
So, I pop the locks on the back doors for some four way fun
Release the curb to a screech I pull off leave my peeps
They got rides of they own, homes to bone they own freaks
Inside the ride their mesmerized sounds bangin' the roof
Black Cadillac Escalade sittin' on deuce, deuce
Catch the whiff of a spiff from a blunt being lit and that's cool...
Cause, I still got some Hennie in the car to hit
So, now its puff, puff pass puff, pours a brother a drink
And it's becoming clear now that I can't clearly think
And my judgment was so that reacted slow
That's when my wheels left the road from the street below
That's when my ride and I decided that we can fly

That's when I instantly sobered up from my high
Later on I then realized I could've avoided this mess
I'm reminded behind the bars and how I cause someone's death

DON'T DRINK AND DRIVE!!!!!!!!

TWO IN ONE...

Another poem inspired by my pastor based on a short
poem he would often times quote during his sermons
entitled Two Natures. I simply wanted to expand in
details the connection with Two Natures as it relates to
my inner struggles. Having the desire to do the right
thing,   but always met with great opposition from the
nature in me that wants nothing to do with saying or
doing what's right (Romans 7:14-23)

THE TALE OF TWO
Written by
Kevin K. King Sr.
(KHARACTER)

I throw caution in the wind now I remove my safety net
For there are two natures inside of me
One so contemptible I detest
The other one is just the opposite and it's this one I love more
Yet they both reside inside of me and are consistently at war

Now the one I hate manipulates, lies, cheats and steals
Is lowdown has no values no shame and no will
It lives to do the wrong thing for that's the only thing it knows
Honesty, you can forget … conniving is the way he goes

Now, the other one simply adores the truth which sometimes
brings on pain
But, knowing this his willingness goes forth to bring on change
He's often ridiculed a lot for the stand he takes
But understands what's at stake and he knows what moves to
make

But that wicked one is a slick he tells me that it's cool
He comes up with all the angles all the excuses says I can't lose
He even paints a picture for me down to its last detail
Then lobbies in my mind so that only that image dwells

His adversary sees this saw it when it began
So he starts to flex his muscles and throws his weight around
again
He bow-guards his way inside then settles in my mind
And quickly begins to speak the truth not wasting anytime

Now, I'd like to say when this occurs more often times than not
That I side with righteousness to make that devil stop
But, truth be told I have indulged with hanging out with that filth
To only have him abandon me and leave me with that guilt...

That guilt that shame that awful pain that comes after the deed
That regret of having disobeyed the word truth tried to heed
So he laughs at me triumphantly for he has found success
Then rightfully brags of victory for impeding my progress

He's a selfish one that thief but, then so too is truth who
continues one his quest to successfully break through
And stubborn!! More than anything he wants to save the day
And refuses to let failure, doubt and pity stand in the way

So, he pulls me from the darkness where the thief wants me to be
Into a realm of light where repentance is set free
And instead of turning me away you know what this one does
Forgives my indiscretions and doubles up on his love

That's something that that wicked one will never ever do
As different as day and night oil and vinegar are these two
But, they have one thing in common and to this I can attest
That they both reside inside of me and beat within my chest

2

MY MOTIVATION...

I never wanted to be successful just for myself. Never! My reasons for wanting success are so that one day I would be able to leave financial securities for my wife and an inheritance for my kids and to be able to help others in need. The origins behind this desire came from seeing how my father, who was a great provider, struggle from paycheck to paycheck just to make sure his family had some of the basic necessities in life. He would often times go out of his way to make sure we had certain amenities not too often afforded to us. This would also mean taking on more responsibilities or for lack of a better word, DEBT. No matter how hard he worked it seemed it was never enough to get him out of the hole. But, I never saw him complain and yet I know he was under some measure of stress. My father wanted for me what I want for my kids and that's to go further and to do better than me and do it the right way. So, as I continue on my journey that's what I strive for to step up the family name and to leave a legacy and inheritance. This is in remembrance of my dad... my, Pops.

DOWN THE LINE
Written by
Kevin K. King Sr.

I wanna break this chain in my family line
Seems like we've always been in a financial bind

Only making enough money to just get by
From paycheck to paycheck time after time

Soon as I make it someone's standing there
With their hand held out looking for their share

And after he gets paid then another comes
Then another one and another one until I'm done

Or until it's done and whatever's left
Must be saved and put towards the next paycheck

And so goes the cycle starting over again
I do the work someone else gets the ends

In a way, I can see why brother slang dope
Maybe envy or motivated by seeing rich folks

Maybe refusing to live in poverty and tired of being broke
Maybe their desires and dream are no different from my hopes

Maybe the working man is a sucker for having a dream
Maybe I'm just a sucker for wanting to earn it clean

And if I'm lucky, I might be able to pay a few bills
If I'm lucky, one day I'll have the house that I will

But, for now things still remain as they do
For me, like my father and maybe his father too

I wanna break this chain in my family line
And be the first one to leave a fortune behind

For my kids and their kids and their kids too
To achieve and succeed at what my dad tried to do

COLOR BLIND...love is love

SOMEWHERE
Written by
Kevin K. King Sr.

Somewhere between meeting you and loving you is where it all began

Somewhere between the color lines and explaining to our family and friends

Somewhere between the looks and stares when we're outside holding hands

Somewhere between the relationship shared between a woman and a man

Somewhere between the phone calls to familiarize ourselves

Somewhere between accepting one another for what's there

Somewhere between the truth and lies to spare one from being hurt

Somewhere between standing strong together for all it's worth

Somewhere between now and then and whatever we've come to share

Somewhere between the two of us in prayer...somewhere

Somewhere between hugging and kissing without us making love

Somewhere between you and I and God up above

COMING TO THE STAGE...

I'm introducing myself to the people. This was me taking a chance on who I was as person and as a poet, confident in what I wanted to say and how I wanted to say it. Trusting my instincts and being free with my thoughts. This is me exploring my personality and having fun doing it.

MY INTRO
Written by
Kevin K. King Sr.
(KHARACTER)

I step up to this stage this mic this night... with confidence, baby
Better yet, call it faith
I don't care what folks think
Your opinions of me whatever it may be will not persuade or affect me in the least
So, any negative comments you can keep
No matter what one may say I'm still gone do this my way
Now, to what folks think traditional poetry is... stop
I come here to kick it up a notch
I come here to help raise the bar and remove any illusions of what poetry methods are
Now, who am I?
I... am... Kharacter
Now, that's a name for me that perfectly fits
Given to me by my wife who insists that should I ever find success with it...
She wants fifty percent
Now, you see I'm a performing poet
And what that means is that sometimes the only way for me to give it to you is to show it win or lose...
Win or lose hit or miss sink or swim or blow it
But, best believe when I leave the stage the name Kharacter... you gone know it
See, I fit the description of my position
I'm a combination of truth, humor, anger, death, sadness and conviction

And my goal is to become the face and to embody each poem I've written

And my aim is your heart no matter its condition, it's my mission and I'm not ashamed

I'm not ashamed to put myself out there for everyone to see

Just like Tom Cruise did in Jerry McGuire when he said, now who's coming with me?

This is your invite and your time and attention is all I desire

This is my intro slash bio into the many shades and side of... Kharacter

And I dare anyone to define me better than I can define myself and be correct because, I'm a bit hard to detect

No, I'm not complex

But, with me you never know what you gone get

So, what I suggest is that you expect the unexpected...

I just suggested...

That you should expect to expect...

When I suggested...

That you expect the unexpected...

I just suggested...

That you should expect to expect...

However, if I suggest that you expect the unexpected I just suggested you should expect to expect then, the unexpected that I just suggested that you should expect to expect is really not unexpected but, then its expect to be expected and not unexpected as originally expected to be unexpected when I suggested that you should expect the unexpected I suggested you should expect to expect

So, what next?

What else could he possibly bring to the table?

What else could he offer to this world of poetry and what's more is he able?

Well, I guess we'll soon see

If my intro slash bio backs up my capability, my ability

I'm unmistakably unique

I'm not a copy of a copy of a copy meaning, I'm not sloppy
I'm and original
So, what I bring to you is my kind of style
It took a while...
For me find out that writing is my gift and that its God sent
So, don't confuse my confidence as arrogance when I speak this, get it untwisted... unravel it
Remove all your assumptions presume nothin'
Let your eyes and ears judge my performance and then determine
If what I say was worth the ink I used put down onto the paper if so, enjoy the show
Go tell a friend
Go across the hall ring the bell knock on the door... tell your neighbor
Invite'em out to a show for themselves to see a variety of stories done though poetry
Hopefully they'll be delighted and intrigued by what they hear and what they see and If not...
Then just do the opposite of everything I just said
Leave your neighbor alone stay at home call it the night go to bed
Or not go to bed
It's your choice, I aint trippin'
Whatever you decided to do is your decision just listen
Because, folks what I'm offering you of just your time and your attention is something wild...
Something strange something new something odd something different
A peek at the life of a man who's not afraid to be himself
See, I'd rather fail being me than to succeed being someone else
So, there you have it
I submit to you my into part bio
And what you see is what you get so cue my arrival
You've been a witness to just a small glimpse of what inside my mind and I wanna thank you...

I wanna thank you for your attention as well as for your time just remember the name... Kharacter

I think it'll be hard for you to forget

Because, as Kharacter I change so you'll never know what I'll do next

PEOPLE CAN BE SO RUDE...

Sometimes without saying a word your silence, can be enough. And it's not just in Chicago.

A CTA BUS PASS
Written by
Kevin K. King Sr.
(KHARACTER)

On a crowded bus there are lots of us all destiny bound
Some standing some sitting quietly only the bus makes a sound
Yet, there's another sound that goes unheard but, physically it's there
It's a foul scent that has been sent that's burning my nose hairs

Now, who done gone and cut one loose who couldn't hold it in?
Who squeezed the cheese and finally decided to break wind?
What nasty sucker broke one off with all of us stuck in here?
Who couldn't wait 'til they got off until the coast was clear?

Who's responsible for my frown and now the water in my eyes?
The sickness I now feel inside the irritation I can't hide
But, no one is gonna volunteer and lay claim to that smell
Of rotten eggs and old cabbage, I hope your butthole swells

Now, everyone is looking around and wondering who it could be
Wondering who in the hell it was that let that funk go free
And everyone's a suspect at this point including me
But, I know I'm not the one but, someone is guilty

Of letting loose this deadly gas that's got me wanting fresh air
I would rather change a baby's diaper because at least I know what's there
But, instead I've got somebody who's grown droppin' bombs off on this bus
Whose only concern is to fart and concern and to hell with all of us

Now, maybe it was that meal they had last night that said oh, no
Maybe they couldn't hold it in and had to let it go
Because, I've been there myself when I was filled with gassy wind
But, I've always found the strength and managed hard to hold it in
So, to me it's inexcusable on a crowded bus to pass gas
This was my experience of a C.T.A bus pass

IN SEARCH OF...Sometimes the most difficult thing to do is nothing

STILL
Written by
Kevin K. King Sr.

There's a reason for us being here
A reason that only God knows
A purpose that's yet been made clear
A destiny yet to unfold

I don't know that reason just yet
Of what that may possibly be
I dare not assume of guess
So I sit back and wait patiently

For no man knows the time
Or the hour we may have left
One should simply focus their mind
And trust Him to order our steps

And lead a life that's pleasing
To the one who gives us mercy and strength
That we may one day hear Him say
Well done though good and faithful servant

QUITE THE DILEMMA...

What do you do when you're on that perfect date on the perfect night with the perfect mood and the perfect setting and then something unexpected... shows up?

THE UNINVITED GUEST
Written by
Kevin K. King Sr.
(KHARACTER)

I met her last week so, tonight's our first date
I reserved a table for two at a real nice place
A candle light dinner in a nice restaurant
I've got my platinum credit card to get whatever I want
I pull out her chair so that she could sit down
Then the maître's does the same for me as I swing around
He hands us two menus then went on to incline
Perhaps a nice drink to sip 'til we dine
We both agreed that this would be fine
What better way for us to unwind
So, he gestures to the waiter who was quick on his time
Who proceeds to retrieve a bottle of red wine
Good mood, good company and a good atmosphere
Everything is perfect, the moment is now here
So, I lean close to share a kiss with my dear
And as I would do so...something strange would appear
What's this? What's this? What's this that I see?
Why, that's a booger hanging out of the nose of this honey
This fine young woman who sits across from me
Is unaware of my stare as I glare at that boogie...
Which jumps out at me like it's in 3-D
And I can't look away so, it may as well be
I can't turn my head now without being rude
And I wish that this was something I could elude but, it's not...
So, I'm stuck just like that thing in her nose
And I could point out this distraction but, then I suppose
That if I did so I really don't know how she would react

How would she respond to me pointing out that booger fact?
What would you do if it were you and you were faced with this dilemma?
What excuse or what signal do I try and give her?
If any at all...or should I just be bold and tell her look...
You've got a booger hanging from your nose
You need to rise from this table and excuse yourself
And go seek a Kleenex out for help or a tissue or a napkin or something you know
But, that uninvited guest of yours has got to go
That party crashing mood changer is a no-no
Just sitting there hanging out killing my flow
Now...that's kind of what I want to say but, not quite to that extreme
Still, this is a delicate situation, you know what I mean?
But, I've got to say something I know I do
Just, how do I go about saying what I need to?
That's the question that faces me on this particular night
I feel no matter what I say it's just not gonna come out right
And honey is looking good too-with the exception of that booger
And to avoid this matter completely well, I would've if I could've but, I can't
And it seems to me that booger is getting bigger and bigger
And I had anticipated a lot this night but this booger I didn't figure...
To be sitting down at this table with us in no way at all
And I know she didn't either and so, now it's my call...
To inform her of this invader that's been preoccupying my time
Yeah, it's true I'm looking at you girl but, it's that booger that's on my mind
It's that booger that's got me tripping out worried about what to do
I've experienced many things on dates but, this is something new
As I sweat this mess with nervousness of what's been place on me
Suddenly, out of nowhere this cutie-pie up's a sneeze!
God, bless you I say, thank you she replies and all I thought was wrong...

Has suddenly been changed into relief because I can see that booger is gone
YOU TALK ABOUT HAPPY!
Now a brother can finally unwind!
And finally get a chance to dine!
And toast with that bottle of red wine!
Because a brother is back to feeling fine!
BUT, WAIT...
She didn't use a napkin when she sneezed
She only used a napkin AFTER the deed
So, now I stop and take things real slow...and wonder
Where in the worldl did that booger go?

AH, TO BE CARE FREE...if only for a moment

JUST CHILL
Written by
Kevin K. King Sr.
(KHARACTER)

Relax...relax...don't take life so serious
Relax...relax...smile some more laugh a lot get delirious
Relax...relax...spend some time with an old friend
Relax...relax...you never know when you'll see them again
You can care for other and their concerns
You can't care more than them it's their lesson to learn
You can be encouraging, supporting and all
But, you can't allow them to cause you to fall
Relax...relax...don't take life so serious
Relax...relax...smile some more laugh a lot get delirious
Relax...relax...spend some time with an old friend
Relax...relax...you never know when you'll see them again
It's like leading a horse to water but, you can't make him drink
You can offer your opinion still they have to think
Relax...relax...don't spend time with a frown
Relax...relax...don't let folks get you down
Do all those things you've been dying to do
Order the most expensive thing off the menu
Actually take that trip you've been dreaming about
Stop making excuses, stop having doubts
Quit stressing situation that will stay the same
Don't worry about stuff that you know you can't change
Quit trying to do more than you're physically able to do
Just relax...relax...relax and worry 'bout you

INSPIRED BY POET, WRITER AND DIRECTOR...Maya Angelou

BEHOLD, BEAUTY
Written by
Kevin K. King Sr.

Some say I'm too fat, they say this because of my shape
Some say I'm too skinny because of my size and weight
You know what I say when I look at what I see
I say behold beauty... because beauty is me

Some say my nose is too wide or that my lips are too big
Some say my nose is too long or that my lips are too thin
It's what I say that counts when I look at what I see
And I say behold beauty... because beauty is me

Some say I'm too light or that my skin is not smooth or fair
Some talk about the color and texture of my hair
Some say I'm so black that I'm too dark to see
I say behold beauty... because beauty is me

Some say I'm not smart because I don't have a degree
Some say that I'm stuck up because I won't give in easily
Some tell me I'm nothing in hope, this they hope I would believe
I say behold beauty... because beauty is me

Some say my clothes are cheap because they're not name brand
Some judge me on this material stand
Some tell me that I'm ugly because they don't like what they see
But, I say behold beauty... because beauty is me

Now, maybe to YOU I'm too fat and that I need to lose weight
Maybe to YOU I'm too skinny because of my size and shape

Or maybe to YOU my nose is too narrow or maybe too wide
Or maybe too YOU my lips are too thin or too big to hide

Maybe too YOU I'm too light and my skin is not smooth and fair
Maybe to YOU I'm too dark and you don't like my hair

Maybe too YOU I'm not smart because I'm not where you are
Maybe to YOU I'm stuck up because I won't go that far

Maybe to YOU my clothes aren't better than yours
And maybe I'm ugly to YOU but, here's one thing for sure
I don't base my life on what you say or think I should be
Here's what I see in the mirror... I see beauty... I see me

ONCE IN A LIFETIME...A magically true moment

THE ENCOUNTER

Written by
Kevin K. King Sr.

Our eyes met
At a time when things weren't meant to be...our eyes met
While he was with you and she was with me
We shared looks of affection during this brief encounter, this brief connection
We exchange mental thoughts and smiles
We embrace in a place forbidden of love all while our eyes keep the company of each other's attention
We begin to speak...with no words being mentioned
Our eyes begin this kind of conversation as we stare
Involving ourselves in this visual love affair...
This feeling we share
Moments of ecstasy...
Moments of pure...visual...intensity
Our minds ponder the possibilities of what this could be...you and me
This feeling of intimacy
I've never experienced anything like this
And to look upon this moment with lust would only cheapen it
This is too rich for that...in fact...it's priceless
And the only reason we can afford this moment...is because our hearts match
Can't deny that there's an attraction between us
But, present company excludes us from holding hands so we just let our eyes touch

Our eyes decide to communicate words that we can't say...in ways that we can't fake...that this...is...fate...
That we should meet...and not meet, speak...and not speak
Yet, this is the way it has to be for you and me
These few stolen moments of secrecy
There's a beauty in this that I see...looking at you...staring at you...
Staring so hard at you it's like I'm trying to see through you...
Trying to feel you...trying to find you...trying to fill my eyes...with you
But, I don't care
I study your face...your eyes...your eyelashes...your eyebrows...your ears...your nose...your lips...your cheeks...your chin
You see, chances are I may not ever see you again after tonight
And you just may be the closest thing to living a dream that I might ever get a chance see again
To be able to remember when I wake and if that's the case
So, I want to take it all in...
Let me stare at you for these brief few moments...
Let me stay in this magical state of transition
Let our eyes stay locked for the these few moments in this...position
Staring at one and other...
Sharing with one and other one of life's few secrets that could never be explained...
And I don't even know your name

Chapter 2

DIRECTION

I'm starting to see now

MY LITTLE ONE...

As much as this was written to encourage my son I believe it was written more to keep me encouraged about my son. "When their young; you carry them in your arms, when their older you carry them in your heart." Unknown

ONE TO GROW ON

Written by
Kevin K. King Sr.

Focus little man and believe as I do
That you can do anything you put your mind to
Focus little man and believe in yourself
And never be afraid to ask someone for help
Focus little man and pay attention in class
Work hard and study so that you can pass
Focus little man for one day you'll see
That when you focus you can achieve

FOR MY SON
Kevin Jr.

I SEE YOU...

My pastor Bishop Horace E. Smith would sometimes ask this question during his sermons "Why are you surprised when the enemy attacks you?" He would then go on to explain and breakdown the reason behind this question saying that it's the enemy's job to try and discourage you so that you'll give up. He would go on to say how the enemy know what God has placed in you and that should you ever become aware of this potential, he know he's in trouble so, he attacks you. He uses people and lies and circumstances to frustrate you to give up. My witness to this came on my job. I had awakened one morning and as I always do, I started my day out with prayer but, this morning was different. When I woke up God immediately told me to go and pray for my boss and supervisor because I was going to be called in for a meeting where I would have to respond to accusations brought on by my supervisor as it pertained to my work performance; or lack thereof. He had even accused me of having poor attendance. All of which weren't true. My first response was what?! Not only was I to lift them up in prayer, but my prayer had to be sincere. I couldn't believe what God was saying to me. I thought, didn't God know what was happening to me on my job. Didn't he know how I was being treated by my supervisor and how he portrayed me to our boss? Matthew chapter 5:44 say, But I say unto you, love your enemies, bless them that curse you, do good to them that hate you, and pray for them which spitefully use you and persecute you. Being obedient, I went into my prayer closet and for nearly an hour I prayed to God calling and lifting up the names of my supervisor and boss asking God to bless them and their families. When I arrived to work that morning just as God had told I was called into the office for a meeting. My supervisor and I sat across from our boss as he ran off a list of the things I allegedly did or didn't do. But, when it was all said and done nothing, NOTHING my supervisor had said was found to be true on any level. My work was justified and my attendance was fine. God's favor was with me. I believe this... that as much as God had me pray for my supervisor and boss, that prayer was really meant to help me to grow. It took me to another level in God of understanding and trusting in Him despite how things look or how I feel and that if God be for you it doesn't matter who's against you. Snakes In The Grass was written to encourage and motivate me as I was going through.

<u>SNAKES IN THE GRASS</u>
Written by
Kevin K. King Sr.

There's a snake in the grass so, watch your step
And it lays there quiet as kept
And when it moves it moves with precision see, it plots to deceive
Don't believe me just ask Eve
See, Eve believed in the words from a snake when it decided to call
Convinced her to eat from the tree causing she and Adam to fall
And to this day, that same snake, it's still around
Except it has legs instead and now it walks the ground
But, I've got news for the snakes in the grass that walk on two feet
Snakes who smile in your face while they lie through their teeth
Snakes that look to devour all that they can
Yeah, I'm aware that you're there so is the strap in my hand
And by strap I don't mean that I'm packing a gun
It's true I am strapped with a weapon but, that's not the one
No, the weapon I use for the task in this case
Is that word of the Lord in the face of a snake
And I'm able to move mountains when I call on His name
I'm able to fight tigers, able to beat Cain
Able to walk through the valley of the shadow of death
And though I stand alone I don't stand by myself, I'm protected by that armor, that word of the Lord
And it's stronger and sharper than any two edge sword
And it'll cut through the heart of a lie just like it should do
And get to the truth behind you so...
A message to the snakes in the grass listen up, this one's for you
The fact that I know who you are well, that's one up for me
And I know where you are and that you lie and deceive
So, I aint afraid of your tactics, those I've come to expect

Or any snares of traps you've set because, here's what I do
I take out that word of the Lord, that sword
I go behind closed doors and cry out 'til my throats sore, my eyes are sore
Because, sometimes the tears don't stop
I pray that God deals with these snakes and the schemes that they plot they tempt me
But, Lord help me to resist the urge to strike back because, if I do that
Then I'm no better than the snakes that attack
And father, help me to relax and let your word come to pass
That the last shall be first and the first shall be last then put in me...
Whatever scriptures or songs it'll take
For me to use when I'm confronted by that venomous snake
That treacherous reptile, that deliberate thief, that poisonous lowdown scoundrel on two feet
See, he doesn't believe he can be defeated and that's his mistake
He can't see that I have a vision and so I walk by faith
And though I get weary at time I won't cease
To keep that word of the Lord within reach
To read that word of the Lord and find peace
And draw strength from that word of the Lord when I'm weak...
Because, after all Father you are my shepherd and I am your sheep
There's a snake in the grass, in fact there's a few
Question is which one are you?

MY BATTLE...

This was...this is me. It speaks of the accounts of the many, many years of drinking and the effect it had on my family. In the beginning as I was writing this I was thinking of a drunk as being funny, I was treating someone who's had a drinking problem as a joke. But, drinking is not a joke. Not in the least. As I was writing The Drunk, God made two things very clear to me the first was that I had to write this from the perspective of my family and how they saw me. The second was that I had to show the drunk. It wouldn't be enough for me to just recite the words, but that I had to act them out as well. This was challenging at first because of how uncomfortable and embarrassing and foolish I felt, but it was those same emotions and experiences that I no doubt put my family through, I had to experience myself. Not to mention the stress and the worry I especially put on my wife and the strain it put on our marriage...BUT, GOD! I'm always reminded of the scripture that best describes to me where I've been, where I could be and where I am Psalm 119:71 (KJV) It is good for me that I have been afflicted; that I might learn thy statues.

THE DRUNK
Written by
Kevin K. King Sr.
(KHARACTER)

I can barely stand, let alone drive
Still don't stop me from getting' in the ride
Still don't stop me from gettin behind the wheel
Even though I know this alcohol has diminished my skills
And I'm reakin' of it too, that and cigarettes
Which seeps through my pours and sits on my breath
Because, I don't know how to drink social and that's my
regret
No, I drink 'til aint nothin' left
Equilibrium is off so, I stumble when I walk
And try as I will I'm unable to stand still
So, I just sway back and forth lean from side to side
I'm well over the limits and you can tell from my eyes…
that I can't see… clearly… and my vision is blurred
And I keep trying to talk too but, my speech is slurred
'Cause in my mind I keep thinking I'm sounding calm and
slick
But, from my mouth I utter words of gibberish

And I'm challengin' folks too, you know, like I wish you would

Liquors got me feelin' mo' harder than it should

But, you can't tell me nothin' see 'cause, I got this

Aint in no position to fight but, I'm still runnin' my lips...

'cause I'm a drunk...and that's what drunks do

Yeah, I'll give you my opinion...I know you didn't ask me to

And I'll keep imposin' my will on folks; I'll keep imposin' my point of view

And I'll give you advice on things when I aint even got a clue

I'm an embarrassment to my family and friends and all those folks who love me so much so...

If you wanna end up like me... then go'head... go'head... drink up

SOMETIMES YOU'VE GOT TO ENCOURAGE YOURSELF...

When you're frustrated, fed up and ready to quit remember...

THE BIG PICUTRE
Written by
Kevin K. King Sr.

You've got me
For five days Monday through Friday if I choose
And you've got me
For those seven of eight hours to use
And you can place me anywhere you want
Tell me where to go and be
And you can switch my time and schedule
To fill some voided need
And you can do this at your discretion
Then claim... *ITS POLICY!*
You draw a vale in front of your true intentions
Attempts to frustrate me
But, it won't work and I'll tell you why
There's favor where I stand
So, I go along with the changes put in place
Because, it's part of a higher plan
Yeah, you've got me... for five days a week
Seven or eight hours to hold
Although it's true that you are in charge
It's GOD who's in control

YOU REAP WHAT YOU SEW...

Sadly, this biblical teaching goes unrecognized by most people both young and old. For those of us who are old enough or wise enough to understand this life principle understand that there are consequences to our actions. What's more disheartening is that our young men and women are given a crash course in this theological saying with sometimes devastating results motivated by their need to fit in and belong to something and more times than not it's something negative and by the end... it's too late. This is such a story.

A KIND OF LOVE
Written by
Kevin K. King Sr.
(KHARACTER)

I guess he's got somethin' to prove
Now that he's been dealin' with some unscrupulous dudes
And he loves to walk around with an attitude
And he loves to hang out and he loves to be rude

And all he loves to do now is get high
Love to wear that hat broke off to the side...
And he loves to roll five or six deep in a ride...
And he loves to be involved when there's a drive by

And he loves to talk crazy to you too... don't he?
Love to talk that talk 'bout what he gone do... don't he?
Love to play hard and disrespect you... don't he?
Love to do this in front of his crew... phony

And he loves to be down when they jump
Love to get you down on the ground, love to kick you, love to stomp you
Love to sit back about it and then brag with his friends
And he'd love to give that love out again so...

I guess he must love runnin' too

Especially loved runnin' when the bullets flew
Loved runnin' hard down that dead end street
Loved bein' snatched and then thrown in the back of a jeep

And he must love surprises too
So much so that they covered his eyes so he couldn't see
through
So much so, that he was excited about the whole ordeal
So much so, that they tied him up just to keep him still

And he must love bein' drivin' to a place
Loved that more than the actual ride and the actual chase
And he must love bein' punched in the face
Must love to finally get the chance to see how the bottom of a
shoe taste

And... he gave out so much love while he lived
So much love that finally love came back with somethin' to give
And he was given so much love that he couldn't catch his
breath
And it was that kind of love that loved him so hard, it loved him
to death

I WAS ASKED BY A FRIEND...

One day a friend of mine asked if I wouldn't mind performing and taking part in a celebration of his parents golden anniversary. He had planned quite the event including a small skit complete with wardrobe. For this occasion I wanted to write something special for them. As a writer it has always been important for me to be honest with myself... to find truth in what I write even if what I write doesn't apply to me directly. So, the question became how can I relate to fifty years of marriage? It would've been easy for me to just throw some words together that sounded sweet and had a nice flow to it and then put it to memory, but how sincere would that have been? Like I said, it is important for me to be true to myself and who I am as a writer. No doubt that at the beginning of my poetry career I would've thrown something together that sounded good, but it's not about the quantity of work that's turned out but the quality of the work that's produced. The way I had to relate to their marriage of fifty years was by relating to my marriage with my wife and putting us in their position of being married for fifty years. I felt that by expressing the love I have for my wife and the love that they have for each other this was the best way for me to be authentic and honest in my presentation to them. Although Without You was written for a wonderful couple for a wonderful occasion, its inspiration came from my connection with my wife.

WITHOUT YOU
Written by
Kevin K. King Sr.

There would be no me without you
There would be no vows made official without saying I do
No surviving the rough times without pulling each other
through
No one able to see me without seeing you

Without you that song wouldn't mean as much
That's why when I hear it I get all choked up
I start to reminisce of a place or a time or a moment we
shared
Seems that song always takes me back there

Because back there is where I met you, first saw you
And I knew I couldn't keep my mind off you I found it so
hard to do
And it's true that when the day would come to an end
I'd get sad until tomorrow when I'd see you again

I couldn't imagine where in this world I would be
without you
Life wouldn't be the same without you
Certainly not as bright without you, wouldn't be right
without you
And I know that I wouldn't be as blessed without you

Because with you I know I could face anything

You're the music that makes my heart sing
If I was down I could just think of you and that would
bring on a smile
For that reason you make it worth while

So, I thank you for saying I do when you did
And I thank you for the gift of life for our kids
And I thank you, for loving me with a love so unique
I thank you for making me complete

MY BETTER HALF...

I understand now when they say opposites attract. You are the lyrics to my music and the words to my poetry. It may sound corny, but you really do complete me.

YET HOLDING ON

Written by
Kevin K. King Sr.

We fit you and I
In the same way as when two hands come together and
the fingers interlock to attach...
You and I fit like that
We connect in ways that has allowed us to share more
than just hearts and minds together...
But, one that has allowed us to share years and time
together
Through whatever the weather permitted we somehow
stayed committed
Nineteen years long
Nineteen years strong
And we yet holding on
And we're gonna keep on keeping on
We endured...
Situations that would've destroyed most couples and in
some cases it has
But, we've got that Ford Truck kind of love that's tough
and built to last

You compliment me in ways that any man would be
proud to call you his wife
You're nice...real nice
You add whatever's missing in my life
Nineteen years long
Nineteen years strong
And we yet holding on
And we're gonna keep on keeping on
You're the plus to my minus
If we were cartoons you'd be that blanket I would need if
my name were Linus
For comfort your relax me, you keep me warm
You assure me when I have doubts and bring peace to
my storm
Whatever it is that I don't know...you do
And whenever I'm feeling down you speak a word to me
that's true
All you really ask of me is to keep you happy
So, I strive to provide you with that basic necessity...trust
me I'm working at it
Nineteen years long
Nineteen years strong
And we yet holding on
And we're gonna keep on keeping on
You're smart and you're savvy...you're tough

You can be hard when you need to be yet, still remain sweet enough
Plus, you're got that good...you know
So, let's make plans for later on to go upstairs and ...you know
See, I can be me around you because, you know who I am
And the fact that you're in my corner make me a very fortunate man
Blessed is what I am
Nineteen year long
Nineteen years strong
And we yet holding on
And with God on our side...we gone keep on keeping on

SELLING WOLF TICKETS...

Sometimes the one with the biggest mouth is usually the biggest coward. Period! There are no two statements I believe more than these (1) Real bad boys move in silence and (2) it's the quiet ones you've got to watch. Folks with big mouths tend to use those big mouths as a scare tactic to intimidate and draw attention. For those who aren't familiar with this method it can be quite effective. But, every now and then Mr. or Mrs. Big Mouth run into that one person who's not intimidated by their loud talking-expletive-flying-big mouths. That one person who doesn't shy away from confrontations and are more than willing to find out just how tough they think they are. That one person, who welcomes the challenge and is willing to shut you up.

SECOND HAND SMOKE
Written by
Kevin K. King Sr.
(KHARACTER)

Every day he be runnin' his mouth, every day
He always got somethin' to say
Bout, what he gone do, what he gone get and what he done did
Bout, who he knows, who he gone get makin' these kinds of threats
And every day, dudes be listenin' to him runnin' his mouth
Goin' around talkin', braggin', laughin' and liein' about...
What he done did to somebody and how he gets down
Yeah, he was always throwin' those kinds of threats around
He was always in the crowd yellin' louder than most
Takin' in mo' air blowin' out mo' smoke
Belivin' his own hype was his first mistake...
His second was throwin' around his weight
But, he figured he could do that because of his size
Yeah, he was a big guy, but nothin' was mo' bigger than them lies
He could make a lot of money off the story he told
If he wrote fiction novels he'd have a million copies sold, but he aint no
writer
And every word that he spoke was smoke
Used to intimidate and impress other folks
He was bitin' off way more than he could possibly chew and swallow,
well...
That was gone be even harder for him to do
But, do it he must to prove he was just that tough
He was gone have to step up and back up that rough stuff that he was
spittin' out daily and he didn't hold back
It was like his mouth got ahold of a pack of ex-lax...'cause he was
runnin' off royally with his lies and threats
He took a deep breath and inhaled mo' smoke in his chest...

And mo' garbage came out and mo' lies were told
And mo' nonsense spewed forth from his mouth and rolled
And mo' stories were said and mo' junk was thrown, but mo'
importantly... mo' smoke was blown
Right into the face of this one kid who done finally had enough
And finally, finally called him out on his bluff
Listen up
To all of my young buck wanna be gangster type thug, niggas you better
know this...
That if you gone play the boss and walk the walk and talk the talk
You better know that everybody you step to aint soft
Because, a real G gone peep game and so, yeah my man peeped his
So, he messed up when he stepped to that one kid
High off his own ego like he was smokin' that loud
But, what stopped him dead in his tracks, what made him calm down
This kid stuck that gun in his face and now it aint no joke
He told him "Say somethin' now, nigger!"
Now all that smoke... made him choke

BUSINESS AS USUAL...something's got to change

RECYCLE
Written by
Kevin K. King Sr.
(Kharacter)

Part of the reason our kids can't get right is because the adults
keep getting wrong
See, we keep preaching to these kids and it's really not what we
preach
But, that we keep preaching the same old song
This is called recycled nonsense
Yet THEY say it's new THEY say it's fixed
THEY say it's working because some parts have been switched
But, first of all that aint new… it's refurbished so as far as being
fixed
The outside just looks good but the inside is the same old
shhhhhh……
See, the outside has just been disguised to hide what's inside of
it
Really, to cover up what's going inside… its true intent
So, words were rearranged in exchange for your common sense
They were recycled then reused then altered a bit
And what's more evident to this in this present time is this
That it's become common practice to sound sincere while
selling you nonsense
Trying to convince you that the nonsense really does make
sense

And they do this by taking the TRUTH and a LIE and then they switch, now stop me if you've heard this...

Leave No Child Behind... let's start with this commitment

How committed are THOSE who started this commitment?

Or is this just another statement with no real substance to it?

Just some recycled word but, don't OUR kids deserve a real commitment to this commitment?

Yet, THEY stress this to the fullest this *Leave No Child Behind*

When year after year it's OUR children who fall behind

It's OUR children who are the majority of kids who never graduate on time

So, when THEY say *Leave No Child Behind* whose child are THEY referring to YOUR child or MINE?

What about HIS child or HERS?

Or better yet the kids in the CITY or the SUBURBS

Because, I've never heard of any suburban schools being closed down or being short on funds when the next school year rolls around

But, when it comes to OUR schools we've got problems and issues

Something is always going on, something is always wrong

It seems that each year that THEY'RE saying a school must be closed because the test scores are low or the attendance is low

So, as far as receiving funds that's out the door

And correct me if I'm wrong but, isn't that what the LOTTERY was for?

It was... until THEY dipped into that pool and recycled that rule, changed it

Then gave what was left to the schools

Yet, THEY keep stressing *Leave No Child Behind*
But, short the funds and materials to educate their minds…
ironic isn't it?
So, it makes me wonder about this commitment
Is it really a commitment or really just a recycled statement?
Something that just looks good on paper and sounds good to
the ear
Yet, the words have been recycled so the truth isn't clear
It's like a contract you never had someone look at but, you
were so excited you just signed on…
When the real truth is in the fine print written too little too long

BETTER THEY THINK YOU A FOOL...

Rather than open your mouth

MR EDUCATIONAL, EDUCATES

Written by
Kevin K. King Sr.
(Kharacter)

Aint nothin' mo' finer than a woman with an education
That's right education, that's... E D D U K A Y S H U N... education
Give me a woman with knowledge and that's all I need
That's right, that's... N A W L E I G E E... knowledge
A woman with style, a woman with class, a woman with, with, with...
intelligence, yeah that's... E N T E L L A J E E N I E N S E S C E...
intelligence JUST... LIKE... ME!
'Cause, I'm goin' nowhere fast and I'm in a hurry to get there

IT'S WHAT I DO...

As much as I love the fit of a good pen in my hand I love
even more the possibilities of what we can create
together stories, scripts, lyrics, poems any of these
things. So, before I finalize anything I've written by typing
it up and saving it to my laptop, it's just me and my pen
doing the work aided by thousands of sheets of paper
and hundreds of bottles of whiteout and you know what,
I love it. Perhaps, more than anything, I love the creative
process I go through of putting letters together to form
words and then those words come together to form
sentences and those sentences turn into things that
capture the hearts and minds of the reader.

I WRITES
Written by
Kevin K. King Sr.
(KHARACTER)

Now, before I was born I was already given this gift in life
Before my conception
Before my moms and pops even made the connection to bring
forth my conception...
I was to be born possein' this gift... I writes
So, excuse my vernacular but...
If you put a pen in my hand then I's dangerous, man... I tell you,
I'm lethal
Why tryin' to duplicate my style is like puttin' out a bad movie
and callin' it a sequel
No, there is no equal... not even for yo' coffee so back off me
There's only one *KHARACTER* in town and I'm it
And every poem is like a role in a play that I fit
And every stage where I come to display my gift is my home
So, yeah I'm comfortable up here it's where I belong... in plain
view
In front of many or a few, in front of thousands or just two
I'm still gone bring it to ya cause that's what I do
See, I'm committed to this life that I spend with my pen to the
point it's a sin...
I need prayer bring a preacher in
Then usher him down to the front and let the healing begin
Then baptize me in ink so that I can start again

I'm a fen to this pen, like Eric B is to the mic
And I'm sorry but, the one person it affects truly is my wife
Because, sometimes I don't really have no headache at night
I just use that as an excuse to go get my pen and write
And sometimes we go at it all night...
Until the early mornin' crack of dawnin' got me yarnin'
Let me wipe the cold from my eyes
To see if I still got my pen by my side
And I'm relentless with it
Consistent as consistent can be when consistently putting
sentences down perfectly... well, properly... well, gradually...
Gradually growing as I write
Gradually showing that I've been blessed by God so, let me
bless this stage this mic
Because, Lord knows that I love to perform on stages
He knows that I love to recite so I write pages and pages of
poetry
Give some music then I'll come lyrically
I'll even sing a little gospel and R&B if need be
See, I come well equipped with my gifts
Therefore I must use them, properly use them, not abuse them
or I'll lose them
That's why whenever I write, wherever I write, whatever I write
it's gotta be right, it's gotta be tight, it's gotta make sense to
the listeners ear, it's gotta be clear
Otherwise what's the point to it if you can't hear?
If you can't understand what I say when I talk...
Then I need to get off this stage and walk
But, the Lord won't let me be lazy, not when it comes to this

He won't let me short change His talents or His gifts
He won't let me just write down anything for the sake of a rhyme
So, I take my time with these lines
Search my mind 'til I find the right words to use
Call me picky if you like but, I prefer being precise about each word that I choose
That, I don't rush to do, I'm too objective
Quite selective in my choice
Because, every word has a meaning I simply provide the voice
You see, I give words life when I write
I breathe life in the word I recite when I step to the mic without question
No if, but's, maybe's, or might
I won't rest the ink in the pen 'til the poem is done right or how I like for my flow to go
Because, sometimes I write quick and sometimes I write slow
Sometimes I stop for a moment to give my brain rest
So many thoughts I've gotta take a break from the process just to give me time enough to relax
Then I'm right back focus, not feelin' hopeless
Ideas are starting to flow once again
So, I grips the pen as I then begin to reacquaint myself with the paper
The lines are just beggin' for me to embrace her, to lace her with the lyrical ink from my pen
To begin this process of writing again
Words rush me but, I gotta slow down I gotta think
In the meantime my pen's so excited it starts to drip ink

It's ready to start turning some words into lines into phrases
So, I can start hittin' some stages and hey...
I just may headline a show one day, you never know...
I could be a success in my own right and headline my own
show, it's possible
Because, this thing is more than just a dream
God has blessed me with the gifts and the means
He put it all in me to be creatively able to write and I don't' take
it for granted, I don't take it for spite...
And I don't take it lightly, not likely you see
This is a God given ability; my best days are ahead of me
Lyrically or otherwise just give me a pen
Give me some time to meditate and concentrate and then
watch the magic begin
Because, me and my pen... we tight
Because, it knows that I won't rush to write what I don't like
It knows that I won't settle for anything less
It trusts me to deliver so, I deliver my best
Now, back to the pen again as I then begin to begin again with
the pen again to begin writing again
Words I write, I often write and rewrite type then retype
And I'll continue this process 'til its right, 'til it's done how I like
I'd be remised if I didn't
I'd be wasting the best of the gift God has given
Therefore, I insist on taking my time with my pen...
With me until the ink ends this pen, equips me aids and assists
me
With lyrics and stories, scripts and poetry
A variety of subjects to choose but, which one should I use?

What's my general mood? What's my attitude?

How should I come off with this one? How should I come off with that?

If in fact the stage is my home then I know the pens got my back

So, I can't afford to come off being lazy, are you crazy?

I've gotta use this gift God gave me daily and keep writing 'til it all comes out

I'm walkin' off this stage like I walked on to it, having no doubts

Knowing that I gave it my all so, I'll have no regrets

I've got potential in areas ya'll aint even seen yet

So, I'm gonna work this 'til there's no more left

And I won't short change what I have nor will I half step

I owe it to myself to be true

That's why I take the time out that I take cause, I'm gone make it do what it do

So, if you don't see me on the scene for a while best believe I've been...

Off on a journey recreating some magic with my pen

So, as I close, as I bring this poem of mine to an end

Let's recall the nature of it all lets' review the relationship of my pen

A brief summary if you will to summarize what I've described as one of the greatest gifts I did receive to which God did provide

I love to write

I could spend hours on one line just to get it right

And I love to type

But, only after I write and only after it's what I like

And I love the nights

When I'm up on stage underneath those stage lights
And I love to recite
Because, I'm comfortable on stage with or without a mic
I love this life I share with my pen
I love this relationship that we're in
I love the reasons why I can describe my pen as my close friend
I write for the love of the art, for the drive
I write from the passion that comes from inside
I write for myself and I'll write this way 'til I die
I love this life, I love the lights, I love the days, and I love the
nights
I love the stage, I love the mic, I love to type, and I must recite
that's why I write

NO ONE PERSON IS BIGGER THAN THE ART OF POETRY...

I always get nervous before I step out on stage. Always. The anticipation of my name being called and the waiting around is enough to make a person go crazy and I've been doing this for over ten years. So, I can imagine how someone who has never performed and never stood before and audience, never recited out loud in front of anyone other than themselves might feel doing all of these things for the first time. It can be quite the experience. Your nerves kick into high gear. You're scared and your emotions are all over the place. You want to make a good impression on the people who are watching. At that moment it's all courage with just a dash of confidence mixed in. Bottom line is... it takes a lot to stand up there so, who are we not to give you the respect of our attention? There's an expression amongst poets that goes "Respect the mic." It's often said out loud to those people in the audience who continue to talk while performers take to the stage to do his or her thing. Yet as poets, we are often times the biggest infraction of this very expression, an expression which simply asks one to keep it quiet... and for the most part the people tend to comply with this request. Whether you're a seasoned vet in the poetry game or a first time cherry on the scene, you deserve to be heard and not interrupted. To be fair I too have been guilty of this same behavior in the past, but have since made a conservative effort of lending the. Still, there are those who are so consumed and fascinated with themselves and their company that they are oblivious to the concept of being respectful to those on stage. They seem to only be interested in their own voice and the voice of those there with. They all share the same mentality and attitude about NOT respecting someone else poetry as if it's not worthy of their attention. So, to those people and people like them this one's for you.

RESPECT THE MIC
Written by
Kevin K. King Sr.
(KHARACTER)

I guess that before you and after you other poets... don't matter which would explain your constant chit-chatter
As you and your crew continue to talk through yet another poet's piece
Only stopping really when it's your turn to speak and then you want peace and quiet...
BECAUSE A REAL POET IS ON THE MIC AND I KNOW THAT IT'S YOUR PLEASURE TO SEE A REAL POET HERE TONIGHT
TO HEAR A REAL POET RECITE SOME REAL POETRY BECAUSE MY POETRY IS REAL TIGHT
AND OUTSIDE OF ME, THERE'S NO OTHER POET OUT HERE THAT CAN DO REAL POETY RIGHT!
And so I guess that's why you talk... you and your crew
Continue to talk through pieces other poets do
Sharing a story or two while laughing along with your crew when really...
More respect is due from a poet as **REAL** as you
Oh, but you're an exception to the rule I guess, that exceptional guest
You don't believe in giving other poets your respect, not unless it's someone you like...
Then you want folks to respect the mic...
It's only when your people are up there that you seem to be to care
Otherwise you just keep on running your mouth
Going around talking about whatever it is you keep on running your mouth off talking about... whatever that is
But, it definitely appears to me to be more important than you respecting another poet's poetry
While they talk you seem to talk even louder
I guess it's cause you've got a crowd around you and maybe you're a star and people should know who you are
You think that you're the coldest poet in history... and that may be
But, you're also the most disrespectful poet that we hear and clearly see
You're rude... all you do is talk
Why don't you take your outside voice outside for a walk?

Because, outside you can talk, talk 'til your heart's content
But, when you're done come back in from outside and sit but, close your lips a bit so that your ears can hear
I know their willing to listen but, can your mouth stand clear to stay closed for a while, while the performer speaks
I know it's hard for you to do... just try to
We just ask that you keep your table talk down some... to a minimum
And let the poets on stage get that attention
But, no I'm still guessing by the way you're still acting that aint gone happen
Just so happens to be you can't hear me
Still want the floor to yourself I see
Still want folks to know who you are... clearly
Still want all the attention on you even while you're sitting down
You still want folks to come and gather around so, I'll tell you what
Let's just take the mic off the stage and bring it down there
Let's take the lights off the stage and shine them down there
Folks, grab your tables and chairs and let's place them right there...
Next to those poets who know it all and are so willing to share their RUD TALK 101... it's their lesson
We're so sorry to be doing poetry during your RUD TALK session
Go on and continue you were trying to say...
No, it's our bag it's our fault we'll be quiet you can talk!
Go on and tell us what we all need to know about how other poets should behave when other poets have the floor
Why, we are just so glad that you even came out here tonight to bless the mic
We should be grateful that you chose this place to recite so, why don't you take the mic and...
You're not reciting... Oh, you've already recited... So, you're just waiting on yo' peeps to get up there... Can I ask you a question?
Where's the love you once had for the love of the art? When did it start? What point did it stop?
At what point did you figure you were above showing respect but, that it should be given to you when you step on to a set?
Because, if that's the case... maybe you need your own poetry stage
A stage where poetry plays for poet's whose way is just like yours or...
Maybe you need your own poetry stand that comes with a mic that sits on a stage with its own poetry lights or...

Maybe you need your own poetry crowd to follow you around and scream your name loud or...
Maybe you need someone to tell you you're cold because that never gets old... someone to pat you on the back and say you're all that or...
Maybe you need someone who... maybe you can get a.... you probably should...
Maybe... you just need a hug
Bottom line is this... stop doing it... stop disrespecting the mic
Stop going on loud talking while other poets recite
Because, despite what you think they deserve to be heard just like you do
Mind your tone as others perform as the show continues
Because, there are other people in here besides you and your crew
And maybe they would like to hear those other poets too so, please respect the mic

A PIECE OF MY MIND...
Sometime you need to get some things off your chest
that have been pressing on you and trying to weight you
down...and that's okay.

TIRED
Written by
Kevin K. King Sr.

I'm tired of business as usual... I'm tired of it
I'm tired of folks complaining about change
Some of the same folks complaining about change aint trying to change one thang!
I'm tired of hearing about yo' progress but, seeing no gain... I'm tired of it
I'm tired of scary folks too
Scary folks who tell you *not to rock the boat cause, we comfortable here...*
Scary folks would rather live beneath their privileges rather than conquer their fears... I'm tired of it
I'm tired of my God given good sense being replaced by man-made laws filled with nonsense... I'm tired of the quick fix
We're putting band-aides on wounds that need to be stitched... I'm tired of it
I'm tired of those folks whose outlook on life is always dim
I'm 'bout tired of him... or her... whoever
Time yo' sun shines here they come with nothing but bad news and even worse weather...I'm tired of it
I'm tired of accepting scraps off someone else's table then told I should be grateful... for what?

Leftover you left over THEN offered them to me as if to say *see, I always look out for my friend...*
Then why didn't you invite me to the table at the beginning of the meal instead of at the end? I'm tired of it
I'm tired of lukewarm folks... I'd rather you'd be hot or cold, forget all that in between
That just means you straddle the fence and that you're afraid to commit
You play both sides and I'm tired of it
I'm tired of parents who don't raise their kids
These are always the same parents talkin' bout what their child aint did
I'm tired of this generational welfare curse on my folks
Got us dependent on assistant like its some form of dope
I'm tired of regulations and rules in public schools that are used as a crutch for those who behave like fools... talkin' bout, *he or she has issues...*
No, doubt some of them do
But, even then that's sometimes used as an excuse... I'm tired of it
I'm tired of ME being an option for you... while YOU are my only option
I'm tired of bad people getting away because good people DON'T SAY NOTHING!
I'm tired of my rights as a parent being controlled by those who don't look how I look, live where I live, walk where I walk, hear what I hear, see what I see, face what I face, fight where I fight, cry where I cry, lay where I lay, know what I know, deal with

what I have to deal with on a daily bases... THEN TRY TO TELL
ME HOW TO RAISE MY KIDS!
I'M TIRED OF IT!

THINGS SURE HAVE CHANGED...

I witnessed firsthand the destructive force and impact gangs and drugs had on my beloved neighborhood (40TH St.) and its surrounding areas. I watched as gangs took over drugs moved in, neighbors moved out, property value went down, apartment buildings closed up, neighborhoods were shut down, city and private developers took over, contractors moved in, new buildings went up while some converted into condominiums. I watched as old faces (blacks) moved out and new faces (white) moved in. I must confess that while writing Face Lift I found myself being very anger and very bitter towards white America. But, as I continued to write I soon realized that the root of my anger had come from the disappointment and sadness I felt at my own people because of our own mistreatment of our environment our culture and more importantly... US.

FACE LIFT
Written by
Kevin K. King Sr.

I see new faces in old places, places I grew up called home
And these faces in old places are faces not of my skin tone
Yet they come from various places these faces to purchases themselves
new spaces
In these vacant places, which have now been renovated...upgraded,
upscale and updated

Now the old the old faces that once stayed in these old places
Had once stayed in spaces that were rather unique places did these
faces
Stay in places with other faces same as their faces in places like their
places but, good Spaces
Soon became run down places
Some were torn down places to make room for new places in there
spaces
And these were some real good places
So good that the new faces wanted to have these spaces

Now, there was a time when there were some vacant places in the new
faces spaces
And these too were said to be some real good places
In fact, some of the old faces tried buying spaces in these vacant places
owned by the new faces
But, some of the new faces didn't want to sell their places to the old
faces so that they could have spaces in their places...
And it wasn't that they lacked the funds to relocate to those places
They did, however lack the texture to occupy those spaces

Now, some plans were put in place for the old faces places
Plans which called for the old faces places to be vacant
And these plans required drugs and gangs to infest these places
Including using help from some old faces
And it was THOSE faces that started destroying places
THOSE faces started making the older faces feel concerned about their spaces
THOSE faces starting taking, shooting and robing places, breaking and burning down their own places so, in came some NEW faces
Then the NEW faces started buying up the rest of the old places
The NEW faces started closing down the rest of the old spaces
The NEW faces started building in those same old places and wouldn't you know it, NEW faces started moving in...
And in came more NEW faces

So, what about the new faces places?
What about those now vacant spaces?
What about the new faces old places and old spaces?
What will they now do with those spaces since they now have more convenient and better places?
Well, the President and Vice President of the New Faces Association sat down to discuss this matter and it kind of went like this...
"Bob, lets sell our spaces to the old faces."
"Rob, you mean those same old faces that wanted to buy our places?"
"Yeah, Bob those faces."
"Okay, Rob that's great and for those that can't afford them let's give them section-eight because, we can control that."
So, the new faces started selling their spaces to the old faces
And the old faces started moving into the new faces old places
Then the new faces started moving into the old faces new places
See, the old faces and new faces trade space
Question...

If the new faces places were such good spaces why aren't the new staying in those places?
Why are the new faces now willing to sell those same places to the same old faces they didn't want in theirs spaces?
Why couldn't they just fix up the old places for the old faces and get rid of those faces that were destroying places?
Why sit back and let places become run down spaces, unless the plan was to have those places?
And they got'em too...

They started turning everything into high class places, condo spaces
No hope for the old faces to return to those places
Sure, you've got some of our faces that can afford those places
But, the majority of our faces have now been section-eight located to other places...suburban spaces
Right next door to THOSE same old faces we didn't want in our places
Because, THOSE faces did more than just trade spaces with the new faces
THOSE faces help destroy their own places
To sum it up it's like this...
See, the old faces they've got new spaces
And the new faces they've got new spaces too
But, here's the difference...
While the new faces new spaces came with new places
The old faces just got new places because, nothing else was new

Chapter 3

PURPOSE

He didn't save me for me; He saved me
to save someone else

MY TESTIMONY...

This is the very first poem I could honestly say was all GOD. I had nothing to do with how it came out, no control over what was being written down or how it was to be written down. This was also the first time I was writing something that I didn't believe or understand and because of this, I hated it. I was angry about it and very bitter. Without question I now know that this was a word from God about taking control of your life, a word to encourage those who were going through a valley, a positive inspirational word. The problem I had with this however was that I was one of those who were going through the valley. I didn't believe in the words myself. The words I was writing down from God. To me, I felt the entire poem was a lie and that God didn't care about the issues that faced me and my family at the time. Every day I would add to this poem words of strength and hope to encourage and inspire and yet, I felt neither encouraged or inspired strengthened or hopeful. But, I continued to move forward pen in hand paper underneath writing and adding to this poem as the things around me, the things that I faced, things that my family faced only got worse. After a few weeks I had finished what God had given me to write and found myself sitting in my room stressed out. I had a lot on my mind... three months behind on my mortgage, my gas was off which meant no running hot water, lights were in danger of being shut off as well as the water and phone bill being way past due, food running low. I found myself in the position of borrowing money from loan places. Soon after I found myself borrowing more money from other loan places to pay back money I had borrowed from those other loan places. I felt as a husband and father that I had let my family down. But, it was a phone call from one of the many bill collectors that sent me over the edge. Not that it was any different from any of the other numerous phone calls I had been receiving previously from bill collectors but, this was just my breaking point. I was just tired. Tired of avoiding the calls, tired of coming up with excuses, tired of making agreements and arrangements and commitments I knew that I couldn't keep. That was just it. Enough is enough. I broke down. I fell to the floor and began to cry uncontrollably first out of pain and then after a while, out of frustration and angry asking God Why?! Why me?! Why don't you help me?! Why don't you help my family? A rage started to rise inside of me that I had never experienced before. One so strong that I began to pound my fist on the floor and against the wall asking God the same questions over and over again why?! I wondered what I did to deserve this. Finally, in my rage my anger I had done the unthinkable... I had cussed God. I called Him a liar... I said I don't believe in you... I told Him I hate you... I told God, I hate you all in anger. The tears were falling so hard and so fast that I couldn't see. After a few minutes, I couldn't cry any more... I couldn't talk. I was physically and mentally drained. Then clear as day I heard God tell me "Now, get up and say that poem". I didn't what to get up. With all that I was feeling and experiencing I didn't want to do anything but, I knew I had to. I knew I had to get up. I didn't know what to feel at that moment, I was numb and God spoken to me again and said "Get up and say that poem". Tears began to fall once again. As I slowly stood up feeling lost and in pain I began to wipe my face... I collected my thoughts... and began to recite these words...

NOTICE OF EVICTION
Written by
Kevin K. King Sr.

I'm cleaning house
And I'm kickin' out Worry, Fear and Doubt
I'm puttin' them all out, they've got to go
They can't room with me no mo'
I've had enough of all the hell they bring
I can't eat, I can't think, I can't rest
Why just the other day while I was trying to get some sleep
I catch Worry sneakin' in stress... I've had enough of this mess
They've been keepin' me up late nights
They've got me pacin' the floors I'm slammin' doors I'm uptight
I don't know if I'm right in my decisions
All I do now is debate
I've become indecisive because Doubt has me unsure of my faith
I tell ya, I done had it up to here
And I'm sick and tired of livin' with Fear
All he's ever done in my life is interfere
I can't keep peace in my life without that clown comin' around
wearin' me down
I once had a smile on my face but, now that's been replaced
Because, Fear discourages me
Makes me unsure of myself
Afraid to pray
Because, it seems to do more harm than help
Afraid to claim what I can do

Because, Fear intimidates me
To the point that I'm even afraid to embrace my own destiny
See, I've been livin' with these three clowns for so long
They've started claimin' my house as their own
And they aint tryin' to leave me alone
And all it took was for trouble to show up to my house
And like trouble… it always shows up unannounced… with bad news to bare
And along with bad news comes hardships and despair
Because, trouble could take you there… but, that's trouble
And that's what trouble's always been about
Always showin' up unannounced
But, see the problem aint trouble because, trouble comes and trouble goes
And trouble's only a problem if you allow trouble to grow, no…
The real issue is these three clowns I've allowed to move in
I've been catchin' hell in my life since then
But, that's it… I've had enough… I aint takin' this no mo'
I'm cleanin' house… and I'm showin' all of these clowns to the door
THEY AINT WELCOM IN HERE!
I'M TIRED OF THE HELL THEY BRING!
I'M TIRED OF THE PROBLEMS THEY CAUSE!
I'M GETTING' RID OF'EM ALL!
I'M PUTTIN' MY HOUSE BACK IN ORDER!
IT WAS MY FAULT IN THE FIRST PLACE FOR ALLOWIN' THEM ACCESS TO MY PLACE!
IT WAS MY FAULT THAT THEY CAME HERE AND STAYED!

IT WAS MY FAULT FOR ALLOWIN' THEM TO TALK WHEN I SHOUL'VE SENT THEM AWAY!
I SHOULD'VE STOPPED THEM BEFORE THEY REACHED MY STAIRS!
I SHOULD'VE CHECKED THEM RIGHT THERE WITH ALL THAT NONSENSE!
FEEDIN' ME NONSENSE!
TELLIN' ME NONSENSE!
HAD ME BELIEVIN' NONSENSE!
AND EVERY SINCE THAT NONSENSE I'VE SINCE HAD TO REPENT!
I've gotten use to livin' a life that was less because I was accepting mess
And I guess that's why Worry kept tryin' to sneak in stress
And I guess that's why Fear felt so comfortable here
And I guess that's why Doubt kept runnin' off at the mouth
But, I'm puttin'em all out now
I've taken all I'm gone take off these three
I'm takin' back what they stole from me
I'm takin' my PEACE back, my LOVE back, my JOY back, my STRENGTH back
I'm takin' my FAITH along with my WORK back, my HOPE back
The GREATER IS HE THAT IS IN ME belief back
And every promise stolen from me, I'm takin' back
My PATIENCE yeah, I'm takin' that back, my KNOWLEDGE in fact
And the WISDOM I've obtained through CHRIST, I'm takin' that back
My HOLY GHOST BOLDNESS to speak the truth, I'm takin' back
And the CONFIDENCE in my WALK and my TALK... all of that

Because, I'm tired of being down... and I'm tired of being depressed
I'm tired of always havin' to feel inadequate
I'm tired of Worry keepin' me woke and Doubt keepin' me stuck
And I'm tired of Fear keepin' me stagnant and afraid to move up
So, I'm servin' this notice of eviction to these three personally
In regards to all the hell that they've been causin' for me
AND I AINT ASKIN' THEM TO LEAVE, EITHER!
Please... I wish I would ASK THEM "Is ya'll ready to go?"
No... I'm puttin' these clowns out my door

A HEAD START...

DURING THE ALTER CALL
Written by
Kevin K. King Sr.
(KHARACTER)

Right after the sermon the alter call was made
For those who want to be saved come down
Don't worry about who's around
This is between you, your soul and God
Yeah, that's him...
That feeling you've been feeling that's been piercing your heart
And as *they* stood, *other folks* stood to
Now, there must've been an alter in the back because that's where
those *other folks* headed to
And it must've been held in the hallways of the foyer
And there must've been ministers back there waiting for them in
prayer
And there must've been a pool in the back with water inside
And it must've been there for those *other folks* who wanted to be
saved and baptized
It must've been... it had to be
Because, see when the alter call was made
Those *other folks* headed down that way
During the alter call...
Just as soon as it was announced
As if on cue did these *other folks* stand and proceed to leave out
Proceed to walk out as if the alter call meant dismissal was
announced...
That these *other folks* gather their things to go
Just as they've done so many times before
During the alter call...
As people were calling on God's name
In need of peace from all of their hurt and pain

These *other folks*…
In the mist of all this thought it simply best to leave… perfect timing
To ease out while folks are crying
During the alter call…
Soon as the pastor opened up the doors to the church
These *other folks* stood up first… to leave
Sometimes before then
Like, right when the people started clapping
Because, to *them* right then right then services came to an end
It was all irrelevant after that
Attentions now turns to being the first one out the seat first out the aisle first to the back first out the door
Because, that's what alter call stood for to those *other folks*
An early start to be the first one to depart
It had no relevance
To *them* it was an insignificant event
Which meant their presence to be present there was just irrelevant
Which meant that since it made no since to sit at an insignificant event of no relevance…
Meant *they* could leave
When those with troubles dared to believe *they*… walked out
Disregarding the importance of what the alter call stood for
What the alter call was about
They took no thought as to what it must be like for those other folks who cried in need of help… in search for a glimpse of hope
No, it didn't bother *them* at all to leave
It didn't matter that folks cried and that some of those folks sat right by their side with tears in their eyes crying, dying inside
No, *they* would just tap them and say excuse me *I'm trying to get by*
I'm trying to leave, quickly leave, vacate, exit before…
I got to beat these folks out the door
I've got no time to take the amount of time its gone take to wait for these folks to have a break through! I can't wait!

Takes to long too!
Why that's an extra fifteen, twenty minutes more I just can't sit for
I only came to hear the pastor preach then I'm gone
That extra ten or fifteen, twenty minutes can be spent gettin' home
I only came to hear the sanctified word of God being preached
After that I got a schedule to keep

So, these *other folks* would leave
In no particular order at all just during the alter call would they do this
Grab their things their belonging and quickly head towards the back
Where the exits were at
It was routine for them to do this, habit I suppose
See, to those *other folks* the alter call wasn't part of the service at all
It was to them merely a gesture from the pastor for those wanting prayer to come up there
Out of the way of those who didn't want to stay
But, I often wonder about those who sat there in their chairs and cried...
As these *other folks* made their way outside
And I often wondered about those who stood there desiring prayer
As these *other folks* walk out that didn't care
And I wondered if it bothered them the way it bothered me to see them leave...
In their time of need so quickly
I wondered if they cared or if it bothered them at all to see them all walk out
I wondered if it caused them to doubt
I hope not...
I hope it didn't stop or discourage them from making their way up to the alter
I hope that they would falter... and come down

And I hope they didn't concern themselves with those *other folks* who for whatever reason couldn't stick around
And God bless them… but let them go, let them leave
If God has you in place in your heart where you dare to believe that He's there
Then rise up from your chairs tears and all… and make your way down to the alter call
And if you're scared… I'll walk with you
As far as those *other folks* reasons for leaving, I don't know
Whatever their reasons for leaving during the alter call they had to go are their reasons me…
I'm staying… believing with you for your breakthrough
And while I'm praying, I'll be praying for those *other folks* too

I MISS YOU, MAN...

At first I thought it best to leave this one out. This is the sum of my relationship with a friend who was tragically taken out of my life and by far one of the more difficult things I've ever written. Demetrius was my best friend. We grew up together in the same neighborhood (40TH ST.) on the same block him on one side of the street and me on the other. We both attended the same high school, Wendell Phillips and since high school with the exception of me going away to the Army, he and I kept the same jobs together no matter where we went. It was like we followed each other. First he got married then I got married. His first child was a girl my first child was a girl and both names started with the letter A. We've always lived close by to one another. We had the same interest, love doing most of the same things. If people saw one of us they would always ask where the other one was, that's how close we were. We were a duo of sorts, if I was Ralph Kramden, he was Ed Norton and we were both silly. Whenever there's a celebration I think of him because I know he would be there celebrating with me. A week before his death we hung out at his place, it was no special occasion that I can recall, just family and friends kicking it and hanging out having a good time on a Saturday night. I would've never thought that one week and one day later, he would be gone, snatched out of my life no see you later, no talk to you soon just... gone. I still recall when I got the phone call of his death from his older brother, in pain, as he could only say to me when I answered the phone "He's gone, man. Meechie's, gone." It didn't register with me at first I couldn't wrap my head around what he was saying and as I heard him go into the details I felt my heart getting heavier and heavier until suddenly I just dropped the phone. I couldn't believe what I was hearing. My wife, who was lying in bed next to me, sat up with a concerned look on her face and asked what's wrong? I didn't know what to say. I didn't know how to answer her. I was just told by my best friend's brother, who was just like my brother, that Demetrius was dead. I couldn't process the information or maybe I just didn't want to. So, she asked me again what was wrong and I told her... Demetrius was dead. Then I got up and walked out of the room. I loved him. He was my brother.

I was at work one day having a hard time handling the death of my friend whose funeral was a few days away when I went into a quiet place to pray. I really needed God to help me get through this. Every passing day seemed to weight more and more on my heart and I felt like I was losing it. Lord, help me, Lord give me a sign that everything is going to be fine. After I had prayed I walked out of that room and into another one where there was a table full of books the job was giving away. As I walked up to this pile of books, sitting on top is this one and the title read Friends Are God Way of Apologizing for Family. Right then a great weight was lifted and I knew God was telling me everything will be fine. This is for the entire Tillman family... I love you all. Love you, Meechie.

MY FRIEND, MY BROTHER
Written by
Kevin K. King Sr.

You were without doubt unique to say the least
Everything about you we'll miss
From your playful and silliness
Right down to that laugh of yours that we couldn't resist
And a party wasn't a party without you knocking something over...and
over...and over
But, until you did then the party really wasn't official
So, it was hard to be upset with you because, that was just you...typical
Man, you'd mess up the best songs around trying to sang
Always changing and adding words and throwing in your name
So, after hearing you sing a song that song would never sound the
same...and so it was
We worked almost every job together, two birds of a feather
From being hired to even quitting...the same time the same day,
together
People would often associate me with you and you with me
So, wherever one was the other one had to be or was at least
asked...where ya, boy?
You made a good time better and a better time...great
So, I'd find it hard to digest for anybody to judge you less...
And if they did disagree they'll have to holla at me...
And we'll calmly sit down and come to agree that THEY don't know
what they're talking about
Because, it was rare to see you upset for long and it was rare to see you
down for long or wearing a frown...
Because, we were both a couple of clowns
But, you...were no one's clown
Still...I've gotta adjust to not having you around

So, I'll cry today just like the days before
And just like the days ahead I'll cry some more
As the weeks and moths go by, birthdays and holidays fly
Just when I think I'm through...somebody
Who I haven't seen in years is gonna come up to me and speak...then ask about you
They'll say "Yo, man what's up, Kev where's ya boy, Meechie at?
Then I'll stop and I'll pause and I'll think...
I'll get that sick feeling back in my stomach again as I recall the absence of my friend
Remembering all of the things that we once did
Now seeing the reflection of your face through your kids
Through your mother...your father...your sisters...Dino
I guess the only peace that I can find in knowing that you're away is believing that you're up there with, Dre
So, I'll tell them you're gone...
I'll explain to them what happened to you so forth and so on
Then we'll shake hands and both go our separate ways
Then I'll smile...now remembering better days
Hearing that voice of yours or you laughing out loud
And if you fly anything like you drive I know you're running into clouds
And maybe then, right then and there I would've found peace
Because, like I said you were unique...
You were like no other
You were not only my best friend...you were my brother
And I love you...I'll miss you...God bless you

WHO'S ASKING?

"Who's speaking to your children?" This was the question posed to the congregation from the pulpit one Sunday from our pastor and it made me think, reflect. Who is speaking to our children? What are they saying to them? How are they being influenced? What role are they playing in your child's life? What did you speak into that child's future? Who's influencing them? Who has their best interest in hand? Life and death are in the power of the tongue: and they that love it shall eat the fruit thereof. Proverbs 18:21 (KJV)

QUESTION IS
Written by
Kevin K. King Sr.

Who told you this is as good as your life is gone get?
Who told you that mess?
Who told you to settle for less?
Who put those ideas in your head?
Who said that you're worthless and that you'll probably
be better off dead?
Who told you to go out and sell drugs instead?
Who told you that is the best way to keep your family
fed?
Who told you that it's okay to be pregnant at thirteen...
to be a mom at fourteen... pregnant again at fifteen?
Who told you to trade in your virginity and give up on
your dream?
Who's responsible for your low self-esteem?
Who's telling our young men to sleep with all the women
you can?
Who said it's just part of you being a man?
Who called you a punks or cowards for deciding to run?
Who told you to stand there and argue with that gun?
Who said since you grew up in the project you're
doomed to fail?

Who told you that the only thing you're fit for is a jail cell?
Who's got you thinking being locked up is cool?
Who said being dumb is acceptable and so is being a fool?
Who told you that you'll never succeed in life so; you may as well stop and go pick a spot on the block and slang rocks?
Who told you that if you gave her your heart that only makes you a wimp?
Who sold you dreams on being hustlers, gangsters and pimps?
Who told you to concentrate on sports so; all you did was play ball?
Who told you, you didn't have to study at all?
Who passed you when you should've failed then told you that it alright?
Who watched you excel on the field then watched you fail in life?
Who told you its okay to be gay?
Who told you its how God made you and that you were born that way?
Who gave permission to Christians to criticize and judge?
Who said God said not to treat you with love?
Who told that you'll end up like your mom, girl and your mom was loose?

Who told you that you'll end up like your dad, boy locked up in a jail suite?
Who told you to blame your environment on the things that you do?
Who said, yeah let that be your excuse?
Who told you to stop trying, stop wasting your time and that you'll never turn out to be much?
Who convince you that life was too tough and that you done had enough and that you should go-head and give your life up?
Who told you this is as good as your life is gone get?
Who's telling our kids all of this mess?

WHEN YOU'RE SICK AND TIRED OF BEING SICK AND TIRED...

This is that I QUIT poem or statement put into a poetic form. After frustrations, disappointments and lies due to work related conditions I wanted to express how I was feeling without actually having to quit. It was very therapeutic. It's me saying to myself stop complaining about your situation and do something about it, make changes upgrade your future. This is more than just a poem to me...it's my motivation.

LETTER OF RESIGINATION
Written by
Kevin K. King Sr.
(Kharacter)

I've gone about as far as I can go in my current job position so
I'm quittin'
Time for me to journey off into a new mission
Because, I've been feelin' stagnant in this position... better yet
useless
It seems the value of my position has become worthless... and I
know my worth
And I'm worth more than this, where I've been
Stuck in a dead in position not growin'
Constantly seein' new people come in and then move up
And there I am stuck
But, I aint blamin' nobody but me
Aint nobody's fault but mine but, I've still got time
I'm gone right this ship
Because, I'm worth more than a few chips of overtime and even
then they short me what's mine
They've got us fiendin' for overtime like...
Pick me! Pick me! Select me! Select me! Choose me! Choose
me! Use me! Use me!
I'm easy... you'll see
You don't even have to kiss me to do me... I'm that easy
We're like crabs in a barrel snatchin' and pullin' and jockin' for
position

Fightin' for work assignments to work
Work that should be given to us first without all of the fuss of
the position
With equal distribution but, it's not
And if this were a movie here would be the plot
An evil corporation that steals from its employees and dares
you to make them stop
This would be the theme song

HUSH LITTLE WORKER DON'T SAY A WORD
I'M NOT GONNA PAY YOU WHAT YOU DESERVE
AND IF YOU COMPLAIN ABOUT WHAT I DO
I'LL GET RID OF YOU

So, I should just be happy to have a job I guess
Happy to settle for less
Happy to let you take from my gross which affects my net; this
determines my paycheck
Which, doesn't' just affect me but, my family
See, I have responsibilities just like you
People... who need me to come through just like you
So, I'm more than offended behind this money business I'm
ticked
And I probably more ticked that you're ticked that I'm ticked
Like I'm not supposes to mention this
Just sit back and let it happen; this continuous nonsense about
my profits
I put in the work... and you withhold from it

The only difference between you and a pimp are the tax-exempts
So, I refuse any longer to be in this job position
Where you receive none of the perks but, all of the criticism and skepticism, cynicism and any other isms
From those who are the most cynical of individuals partial to the truth
Ask them a question about your money and they'll say... "I'll get back to you" ... but, they never do
So, let this poem serve as my letter of resignation
Servin' you notice that in two weeks I'll be leavin' this situation
No... as a matter of fact scratch that; let's just say that today makes two weeks
So, that's it... I quit
Because I deserve better treatment... than this

WHO ARE YOU TRYING TO IMPRESS...REALLY?

At one point I found myself writing with one goal in mind and that goal was trying to please people. Every word that I put down as a poet was a word geared towards impressing folks, trying to wow them with my creative writing skills. I was motivated by the applause I would receive from the crowd both before and after I'd leave the stage and by the notoriety I was starting to receive from amongst my peers as they'd mention my name and pay me complements. I was DRIVEN by popularity and recognition. It was all about me and making a name for myself. It was all about acceptance, fitting in and being embraced by people. It was all about pleasing MAN. Then one day I picked up my pen and pad and began working on another poem. I had gotten six or seven lines into it when suddenly, I drew a blank. Nothing was coming out. I sat there a few seconds then the seconds turned into minutes and still nothing and so I decided to take a little break to clear my mind that and I were a bit frustrated as well. When I returned to the pen and pad after about half hour or so I attempt to try writing again but, quickly found that my problem still persisted. No matter how much I tried nothing came to me, no ink flowed from my pen onto the paper beneath it and when it did I didn't like what I'd written. I didn't trust it. Now, I started to second guess myself at every turn saying this isn't good, that's not good, that's not what I want to say. Over and over again this continued until I eventually tore the pages out and started again. My frustrations mounted as more seconds turned into more minutes and the minutes turned into hours and before you know it, days and then weeks. It was at this point that my frustrations turned into worry and concern. I felt lost. I didn't know what was going on with me. What normally came so natural, almost with ease, was suddenly gone. My spirit was down and in this state of sadness I asked God, what's going on? What's happened to my gift? For years I had been trying to find my place in the world. I use to always wonder how people knew what they were meant to be doing. How did Michael Jordan know that he was supposed to play basketball? How did Denzel Washington know that he was supposed to be an actor? How did Patti Labelle know that she was supposed to be a singer? I wondered about this because these people were and are great in their profession so, this was very important to me because for years the one thing I did more than anything was writing. It was my escape and my peace, something I did all the time and I loved doing. I did it without the wherewithal of purpose or cause or trying to impress people. I just knew I wanted to create something beautiful to share with the world. So, to suddenly have this one thing I loved to do cut off left me feeling useless which lead me to the ask God what's happened to my gift? God responded to me with a question of his own when he asked me who you are trying to please. This was one of those moments where my pastor would say "Say ouch or amen." This was defiantly an Ouch moment for me. With that I took a long hard look at myself and I didn't like who and what I had become and decided at that moment to remove myself off the poetry scene. It was during this time I sought a closer relationship with God and reevaluated my priorities. When I finally reemerged back on the scene after nearly a year I understood my PURPOSE. God had to show me that He's the reason for my gifts and talents. He pulled me out of the lime-light so to speak, to rid me of the ME mentality. I realized that it's NOT about pleasing man but, most definitely about pleasing GOD and keeping him first and from that experience came Writher's Block.

WRITER'S BLOCK
Written by
Kevin K. King Sr.

I realize that God has a divine plan in my life
I realized this one night as I sat down to write... I struggled
Seemed I couldn't get ahold of my thoughts, I felt lost
As if my creative side was cut off
Words had escaped me, eluded me where as once before...
I could just put words on paper until my fingers got sore
Now, I just stare at the paper until an idea is born
Now, I just sit holding my pen until a sentence is formed but, no luck
I can't buy a thought, I can't buy an idea
I can't seem to break through to where my mind is clear
Clouds interfere and it becomes all too apparent
Because, in the middle of my thoughts they move in then my mind
stops sharing with my hand
This in turns stops moving my pen
Which in turns leaves me on the outside looking in and it's got me
wondering...
What's happened to my gift? Where's it gone?
It has me questioning my ability to write like, what's wrong
What's going on inside of me that's got me unable to be the me that I
need to be able to be creatively?
I see signs of my ability periodically
I catch moments from me of what could very well be a possibility... that
I'm coming out of this writer's block soon
Harmony is about to return and that I'll soon be in tune with myself
again
But, as soon as I think the problem's solved
I draw a blank and now I can't seem to recall

Memory stalls and can't seem to gather my thoughts at all
It's as if creatively my creativity has been placed on pause
God, what is this?
Because, this has been going on for too long
I couldn't complete my own thoughts, let alone a full poem
I second guess myself with each line and each time I'd write down one
line I'd white it out only to find...
I had it right the first time... or was it the second?
I don't know, I'm still guessing, so now I just start messing with
everything I wrote now
Uncertain about it all
I get frustrated and take the paper and turn it into a ball
I trash the sheet then grab another one still my thoughts can't be
reached
So, I add this one to the pile on the floor marked incomplete
I'm this far from going off, I'm this close so ready to cuss
Until God tells me to *slow things up*
He said, *what's your rush?*
*What's your hurry? What are you trying to prove? Who blessed you
with those gifts you use? Who?*
*Who gave the talent to create and write? Who called you to be one of
my lights?*
Your writer's block is intentional, all to get you to see
That somewhere along the road you stop acknowledging me
You started putting your gifts first, gifts that I gave
Then you put me second in line behind that which I made
You went off doing your own thing, writing what you wanted to
Writing for man's approval and man's opinion of you
When I called you, I blessed you, I gave you those gifts
I put the words that you speak inside of you that come from your lips
I AM THAT GIFT THAT YOU'VE NEGLECTED TO BE WITH!
*Oh, you think you're just gonna use me for my gifts and just do as you
wish?*

All that I blessed you with, it wasn't just for yourself
I didn't save you for you I saved you to save someone else
But, you went off seeking fortune and fame
You got off the path that I placed you... to busy trying to make a name
for yourself...
You started getting full of yourself
You started making moves without me, you got ahead of yourself
You neglected me because you felt like you can do this yourself but,
neglecting me... is just neglecting my help
So, I said fine...
If you don't need my help then you don't need my gift...
So, I'll take them back along with my abilities to perform them with
And I guess you don't need my directions to guide you through the
nonsense...
So, I'll take those back along with the protection I provide you with
And I guess you don't need me to bless you since you're so full of
yourself...
Discarding my help... more concerned with recognition and wealth...
More concerned with WHO sees you that WHO feed you
Always trying to please man and not me... using my abilities
So, I'll take back ALL that I blessed you with because if I can't be first
Nothing you try and write will work
Who do you think you are?
I'm GOD... Elohim, El Shaddai, Jehovah Jireh
I'm in control of all of this
I'm the one who's responsible for all of your talents and gifts
I placed my hands upon your hands as you began to write
I gave you courage and confidence to stand bold and recite
I lit that fire inside of you, I put that passion inside
I gave you power to speak and to make those words come alive
I could've chosen any vessel but, I intentionally chose you
I could've poured into them all that I poured into
But, I made you specific it was all by design

When I gave you those gifts and talents I had a purpose in mind
NOT for you to take credit for all of my gifts
NOT for you to simply use them as you saw fit
You took for granted my gifts... where they come from... who's they
are... who they belong to... who's in control and in charge
You forgot that you are where you are thus far because of me as
opposed to where I could allow you to be...
And I could allow you to be far from me
Far from my mercy and grace
Far from my covering and far from my face
Far from my favor, my blessings and love
And should I choose... far from those gifts that I gave you that you're so
fund of
Far from it all... if that indeed is what I wanted to do
But, you were predestined by me... I placed an anointing on you
So, son keep your heart and mind on me... keep me first above all
because I WILL NOT be your second option
Keep me even above your family... and you'll see
That much more will I bless you abundantly... trust me
Now, pick up your pen and write... your writer's block has now been
removed

BOTTOMS OUT...

There's an expression called saggin', it's where the pants aren't pulled completely up over the posterior therefore causing them to sag off the bottom and or rear-end. It's a type of style that's become fashionable for young males to adopt, a term and style whose origins come from any prison in America and maybe even abroad.

From what I gather, in prison, there are two reasons for this style of wear (1) the style of the pants saggin' is really not a style at all but as a result of inmates not being able to have belts while incarcerated thereby causing there pants to sag and (2) having your pants saggin' in prison is a sign to other inmates that you are either someone's property, sexually or that you're available for sex all together. In any case our young men walk around freely displaying this look and they seem to do so with great pride and enjoyment. Now, I don't know if they're aware of this style of dress and its meaning but, I do believe however, that this information has been shared and spread around enough over the years that it had to have caught their ears at some point. Once, while at an African festival, I saw these two large posters displaying images of young black men wearing saggy pants with a caption written underneath each explaining its derogatory image. I also read newspaper articles that went into great detail explaining saggin' pants and how it started in prison with inmates, the who, what, where, when and why reasoning of it all complete with quotes and comments from prison inmates both past and present on the meaning of this style and what it represents. In each, they both lead to the same conclusion about saggin' and what it means...SEX. Yet, our young black men seem committed to this look and undeterred by its meaning or by the requests of others who plead with them to pull their pants up citing for themselves this style as...*fashion*. There are images of saggin' everywhere and these images will continue to be at the forefront of our society and on the minds of our young *black men* as long as we continue to promote such images in movies, magazines, television, through celebrities and as long as they continue to go in and out of any prison in America.

Written by
Kevin K. King Sr.
(Kharacter)

Apparently they love to leave the booty out
No, really they don't mind, they don't care about havin' the booty out there so...
Welcome to the peep show
There's no charge, it's a free show
They don't mind if you see 'cause, yo, that's why they wear what they wear the way they wear it so you can see more of their assets...partially dressed
Which they then position, in a position to leave the booty out sittin'
Hangin' over their jeans or sweats
Where they've become more than comfortable in this position to let the buttocks rest
Why, to tell you the truth, I'm actually amazed by the steps they take
The deliberate measure to actually pull the pants below the waist
To actually fix them, adjust them to stay as if to say...
That's it!
That's the position I want them to be!
That's the view I want them to see!
That's my booty!
Protruding over the top of my jeans, peeking from underneath that long, long shirt that I wear...
That's my derriere you're seein"!
It's by design, there's no mistake, I meant to do it, I love walkin' around this way
So, yeah they leave the booty out intentionally to see
And the fact that they do this intentionally is what's so incredible to me
Not that they do it so much but, that they actually thought it out

They thought about how much booty to leave out
They thought about how to position it to stand out
They thought it over, as if they were standing in a mirror going...
"Hum, let me look, let me see, how should I position my booty?"
They thought about it then committed to wearin'em like this
Why, some have even developed themselves a little male switch
I tell you, they insist on wearin' like this
They'd much prefer that the waist line of the pants straddles the hips
They'd prefer this loose fit it seems
They'd much prefer to let the buttock sit on the top of those jeans
while wearing that long, long shirt that seems to come all the way
down
In the same fashion as a girl when she wears that long, long blouse
In the same sense that it complements what she wears
So, I guess in the same sense of a fashion sense guys are looking for
booty complements
Or at the very least recognition... because, after all they say its fashion
But, what kind of fashion for men spotlights the backend?
Call it semi male fashion then
You can call it semi male fashion booty flashin' for men minus the skin
because, it's advertised as such
You tell me...
Why else would guys walk around voluntarily advertising the butt?
Why?
Because it's a peep show
Where pretty much anything goes
Where you can see pants hangin' a little or hangin' all the way low
Why, you can see'em hang down at the halfway, trust me they'll stay
They'll make the adjustments to make sure that the booty stay on
display
They know how to loosen the belt up or even tighten it to fit
They know how to make sure that the booty stays outside the pants to
sit

They know how to place it so that no matter what, you'll still be able to see a view of the booty...
From any angle any position, easily
They do all of this at the peep show...
Where here
You'll see guys who love to advertise the backside for free
All at the peep show...
Where here
You'll see, guys of every shape and every size almost every ethnicity
All at the peep show
Where here
You'll see guys who need no belts at all flash those boxer or brief draws
All come willingly, come baring their booties for free
At the peep show
Where there are no I.D.'s a required for this
There are no tickets needed to purchase for the viewing of this
There are no age limits, no permits, nothing specific for this exhibit
Just some guys willing to showcase the backside
Why, they've got peep shows all over the place
And chances are... you've seen'em
In fact, they may be sitting close by right now
I just want to make them feel comfortable and welcome them and you to the peep show
Oh, I almost forgot... this is an open-end-vatation

THE BLAME GAME...

POINT THE FINGER
Written by
Kevin K. King Sr.
(Kharacter)

Everybody wanna blame the kids
They wanna say this and say that, they wanna complain when in fact
kids... only do what you allow them to do
So, if you wanna blame someone point the finger at you
Now, in case you don't know who you are let me help you
YOU... the one who'd rather be your child's friend and kick it with them
socializing trying hard to fit in... when they don't need you as a partner
or another one of their friends
YOU... the one who every other word out of your mouth is a cuss word
So growing up that's all that child heard
That's why it's now problem for them to cuss up a storm
It's not unusual to them it's the norm
YOU... the negative talkin' name callin' tongue lashin' bashin' assassin
Your affect are every lastin'
Whoever told you that names don't hurt told you a lie
Names can destroy ones will... names can get one killed
YOU... the gang bangin' parent OR parents, that's plural more than one
Meaning you're twice as dumb
Whereas most parents try to keep their kids from joining a gang
You actually encourage being down with those lames
YOU... the drinker and yeah, I've had my hands in that mess
For years my kids had to see me in states of drunkenness
Yet, we want them to respect us and do as we say while we're out
there drunk on display
YOU... the abuser, you speak with your hands and fists
More with the foot that you used on your child to stomp them with
More for kicks

And for punishment just to show them who's boss
Broken arms and black-eyes you later claim no knowledge about
YOU... the excuser, you cover up much
You're always there with excuses whenever your child messes up
You're their crutch
And you're always singing that same old song about how my baby aint done nothin' wrong
YOU... the one who's too busy to take time out to spend with your child
It's no wonder they run wild
It's no wonder you don't know what's going on in your own home
Because, you're hardly there when they're there... and their in there gettin' it on
YOU... the one who gets high in front of his kids and oh, well I guess it is what it is
But, now your kid is getting high with you and now your kid is just as messed up as you
YOU... the addict, your addictions come first
You'll sell your kid if you had to just to fulfill your thirst
You'll sell their future and any hopes and dreams they may have just so you can get that fix... that needle or pipe to hit
YOU... the molester, the incest degenerate
How could you sexually mess with the child that you're suppose to protect?
How could you cradle them in your arms then later betray their trust for wicked lust?
You're the worst... I count you lower than dirt
Yet, WE call them names... WE abuse them... WE cuss them out
WE tell them things to their faces like "You'll never amount to anything"
WE fondled them while locked away in their room
WE involved them in gang life to help end life soon
WE show them things like getting drunk and high and told them it was okay

WE covered up there their mistakes instead of showing them the way
WE embarrassed them on how WE behaved
WE DID THIS! THE ADULTS!
Sad but, it's true
So, if you wanna blame someone point the finger at YOU

IF THE SHOE FITS...

I was encouraged, driven, to be a voice for all of the young men locked up, struggling out in the streets caught up in that gang life and forced to live and do things as a kid because they weren't afforded the luxury of having a father in their lives to help guide and show them the right way. <u>NOT</u> because the mother wouldn't let them be involved in their child's life, <u>NOT</u> because they weren't worthy to be loved by their fathers, <u>NOT</u> through any fault of their own but, simply because the fathers themselves are COWARDS! They chose to run away from their responsibilities. It was their decision to not be involved in raising that child or those children THEY fathered. And that is the true crime. So, this is for all of those mothers who have been struggling and DOING the job of raising these young men, OUR, young men as best they can either with some sort of help or assistance or just on their own. This is for all of the young men and young women who have suffered and are still suffering greatly because of their father's selfish decision to be absent in their lives. This is for all of those who stepped in and pick up the slack because of those men or better yet, BOYS that didn't. Because we understand that it's not their fault. This is supposed to do whatever it's supposed to do to those it applies to...as my pastor would say "Say, ouch or amen."

A FED UP FATHER
Written by
Kevin K. King Sr.

You cat's done made my job harder
I'm talking about all of you absentee father... runaway fathers... no showing up for nothing fathers who don't bother taking hold of their sons
And raising them til the job is done
You marks make me sick... COWARDS! SPERM DONORS!
You don't own up to the responsibilities of raising your seed
That's blood of your blood flesh of your flesh
But, you cowards got up and left because, you want to be street hustlers... street runners... gang soldiers
You've got no right being called a father!
Out there doing that nonsense other cats tell you to do like a fool
It's like the blind leading the blind with no rules
Yeah, you cat's done made my job harder
Because, not only do I have to deal with my two I've got to deal with yours too... and they've got issues
All because you aint been around
And you aint locked up either, you're just to low down
Even if you were locked up so, what I'm not giving you no pass
Locked up for stealing from somebody who had
Too lazy to work for what you could've had
But, you can spend all day scheming on how to get by and all night hanging out getting' high
Yeah, I've got a problem with you cowards calling yourselves fathers
What kind of man would leave his son to be raised by his mother... and nothing's wrong with you?
Nobody's stopping you from doing for that child what it is you need to do, you just choose not to... YOU COWARD!
What's wrong with you?

Oh, but you've got no problem claiming them on that W2
You give real men a bad name
You're the reason for my shame and why they judge all black men the same based on you cowards and lames
Yeah, I blame you for this mess
Got your sons out there fatherless involved in that street life nonsense while you work your same routine of being unseen and unheard from
An absentee run away no showing up for nothing bum
Yeah, you Mr. I'd rather run than to stand than and be accountable to my daughter of son
So, you left it all on the mom to do... coward you
To play the role of a man a job that you're supposed to do
Now, she has to be bothered with being both mother and father because, you're to selfish to be bothered with the kids that you bothered to father
You're right, I am pissed
You had a job you quit an assignment you've failed
That's why so many of our young men are in jail because you've bailed on them
You left them alone to fend for themselves
Yeah, mom was there but, there's nothing like having his father around for help
And maybe that's why our young men can't talk without... smackin' their lips
And maybe that's why some of them can't walk without... having that switch
And maybe that's why our young girls don't have much to choose from
And maybe that's why they find love... in another girls arms, I don't know and I don't care... all I'm saying it this
That if you're not in a comma or dead you're dead wrong
So, all of those excuses you've been using for year you can gone get the hell on
Like I told you early on... I'm not giving you a pass

This has been a message, from a fed up father to all of you dead beat-good for nothing- low down- low life-selfish-useless-inmature-gutless-lazy-heartless-irresponsible-hideaway-no child support paying-cowardly- cheap-no job seeking-no accountability-absentee-runaway-no showing up for nothing- bums
And you know who you are

WHAT IS YOUR WORTH?

I've seen women, beautiful women; highly educated women push for the highest positions in their professions... turn around and SETTLE when it comes to their personal lives.

RENT
Written by
Kevin K. King Sr.

WANTED

Female of any color or ethnicity willing to be cheaply used; Someone to have kids out of wedlock; Must be more than happy being the live in girlfriend or baby's momma or both for long periods of time; Someone of low standards; Willing to settle for much less than what they are worth and deserve and have NO high expectations; Someone to move in and share expenses and do 95% of all house hold chores such as cooking, cleaning, washing, etc., etc.; Someone more than comfortable playing the role of wife, without ever receiving any actual commitment of marriage, SEX IS A MUST! (Low self-esteem a plus); If this is you...

Yeah, I know it sounds crazy but, believe it or not
Many women have gladly accepted taking up this spot, this position
They've already gone on to sign on to be Mrs. I'm Not Worthy To Bare His Name
Official
Still in the dating stage
Five years or more of being engaged but, indulging in martial ways, that's if you're even lucky to be engaged...
Some have only received a promise to this effect which still hasn't happened yet
You're still single
You're still waiting around to see if quite possibility he'll make you his... promise to be
So, with that you move in with him based on that promise to possibly be his... promise to be
And yet, years later still no engagement yet, you have been engaging in much sexual activities
So, the only real promise that has truly taken place is one of promiscuity
They've decide, I'll move in with you with no commitment and share expenses...
I'll have sex with you on regular bases in an instant with no commitment...
Why, I'll even have kids for you with no commitment...
Even if you leave me
I'll still agree to do this so...
Yes... I'm for rent... you can rent me

So, I guess the question would have to be...
Why buy the cow... when you can get the milk for free?
Yes, I'm for rent
And as a rental I completely understand this agreement
You want a relationship, nothing serious, where you're tide down to any real commitment
One with a clause in it that says that you can leave me in an instant when things start to get hectic... I got you, Boo!
You want a relationship, where you can describe me to others as being yo' shawty or yo' girl or yo' baby's momma
Not one where you would have the pleasure of introducing them to me as being your wife or as your child's mother... I got you, Boo!
You want a rental...
One who works cooks and cleans
One who affords you all the luxuries of the bedroom scene... A STRAIGHT RENTAL!
I got you, Boo!
No commitment at all!
No one concrete to keep just a rental, a lease so, I knew you we're searching for me
I knew it from the moment I heard you use the word cheaply, I knew that qualified me
I knew that if I lowered my standards you'd make an offer to me, I knew this...
I knew that if I rearranged my priorities stepped away from integrity and downgraded my quality then, you'd want me...
Because, now I'd be willing to settle for less
Yes, I'm for rent... and I'm cheap
For your very least you'll get my very best
Yeah, rent me...
And for the low, low price of whatever you offer me I'll be what you need me to be
See, I'm not only cheap but, I'm easy to please
Easy to believe whatever you tell me just as long as you'll have me, desperately lonely for affection... *and* I'm cute
Plus, I've got those low self-esteem qualities too
All the insecurities I have they all play into this
Self-consciousness of ME... so, it's ME that I rent

I'll even share you if I have too, for you... that's money well spent... or saved... either way
But, I am what you're looking for, check the records...
My resume, incredible, qualifications, impeccable... my standards, adjustable...
And as far as my time, Boo it's whatever you wanna do... I'm flexible
Why, you'll be hard pressed to find someone more willing to settle for less than me
So, you see; I don't mind being rented
I accept all of the terms and conditions do all the chores that were mentioned
I agree... to a clause to not prevent you to leave should things get heavy... I agree to this
I have no problem with it
I agree to move in with you AND share expenses...
I've got no problem with this at all I understand being rented
I understand the demands that come with having this position
And the prestige honor of being Mrs. I'm Not Worthy To Bare His Name Official
I agree to be your girlfriend for long periods of time, whatever it takes
I'm in no hurry I've got time to wait
You can refer to me to others as being yo' shawty or yo' girl or yo' baby's momma
That doesn't bother me I'm not with all the drama...
And speaking of drama...
I'm not an actress but, I can portray being your wife
I can afford you all of the luxuries in the bedroom at night
Engaged or not it won't stop me from acting out the wife duties of sex...
And since it's a must I'll give you more than enough
As far as having kids out of wedlock... count me I'm in
Sign me up for the position and let the renting begin
I'll bare children for you...
We ain't gotta be married in order for me to carry around a child or two for you
I'll be yo' baby's momma as long as the daddy is you
I told you, I've got you, Boo I understand it... I do
YO' BABY'S MOMMA; PERIOD!
Nothing more serious... because, a mother and father who are married, that's too much of a commitment...
And I know how you feel about that
So you see...
YOU SEE...

All of the benefits that you'll receive just for renting me
I'm a bargain...
A steal...
A low cost participant...
And I can be yours for next to nothing
And I'm available... ... ... I'm for rent

December 4, 2012

PLEASE, REMAIN STANDING...

RESERVED
Written by
Kevin K. King Sr.

It took a lot for her to come here
As she stood outside the church doors she had never come this far before
She was nervous, scared, but she was there now all she had to do was walk in
She had her best clothes on too
And by best meant this purple outfit somewhat short with a tight fit
But, it was hers… it was what she wore… all she had… all she owned
AND it was clean
Much how SHE wanted to be
She was in pain… and had been that way for a while now
And it was this pain along with the shame that kept her from reaching out
Kept her afraid of being embarrassed, afraid of the looks of harassment afraid she'd be judged and that she wouldn't be accepted
Ah, but see this time was different…
She must've stayed up all night fighting her fears determined to make it here and she made it
She pushed her way through it…
Through all of the nonsense trying to stop her
Trying to discourage and block her and got through it
And that was a victory in itself
And it was that feeling she rode all the way to church to seek help
It was THAT feeling, a feeling which she played over and over again in her head
Probably from the first moment that she rose from her bed… then rolled out of bed… then rose to her legs… hen rose to her feet
Showered then changed then made her way up the street
Down to the place that she was excited to see

A place where she felt she would be set free
A place she wanted to be
And as the doors of the church swung open she walked in
And on her face she wore a grin, she couldn't help it
She was both nervous and excited
It was a new day for her, a fresh start, a new beginning… hope
This was the reason for all the grinning
So, she started down the aisle wearing that smile
Near the front she saw a seat she could take, an available space
And as she approached the seat to sit down she was told… wait
Someone was sitting there
So laid a coat on the chair
She said "Okay" with a smile looked around a little while for another place to sit and quickly found it
Same aisle only two rows back was a seat
Right in the middle a nice place to watch the pastor preach
So, as she excused and pardons her way pass some folks heading down to that chair to have a seat there
A woman who was sitting nearby looked her right in the eyes and said… that seat was occupied
And there on the chair… was a jacket
Again she smiled and said "Okay" and made her way from that row she looked to her left and saw another place to go
She saw another seat that was empty another place to sit down so she began to make her way around
She passed a few folks on her way to that seat
And she smiled as she spoke to those folks she would meet however brief the greeting was…
Whether or not they spoke back it simply wasn't an issue with her…
Nor were the fears or worries she carried… she didn't care
Her biggest step was already taken and that step was getting there
Still enthused just by the thought of being in church
Has kept her mind off her pain and hurt
She was gonna get to that chair and sit down in that seat and hear a word from God being preached

And as she drew near to the chair there she saw a hat… a brown hat
In place of where someone normally sat
And it was there as a reminder, a kind of a sign to folks, a kind of a
letter…
I'm not gone; I'm still here, kind of a note
And just in case that message didn't come across clear
It was still relayed verbally by someone who sat near
Oh, well she concluded "Let me see, let me see, let me see" she said
softly
As she looked around sharply
"Where can I sit?" was the question she had asked under her breath
Then to her left was a section
So, she headed in that direction
In between two people there was a seat vacant
And without hesitation she headed towards that location
And as far as she could see, at least from where she stood
There was no one was sitting there as often times there would
But, when she approached that vacant space a book sat in it's placed
So, she inquired about the chair to the two who were sitting there and
asked them "Is that seat being used?"
To which they responded by saying yes were holding this for a guest
She smiled, raised her eyebrows and said "Okay" again
Proceeded then to look around for another seat to sit in
She spots a chair and excitedly she turned her attention there
And started moving rather quickly as if there was no time to spare
A nice place too, she thought and couldn't believe it to be so
Yet, there it was a seat up front which appeared available
For all she knows, despite the woman standing there, the seat was free
And she wanted to be excited about that possibility
But, she was cautious to get excited about the seat that she saw
She was hesitant to let her feelings become so emotionally drawn
But, she couldn't help it
She tried to contain it, she were but a few feet away
But, close enough to hear someone say… it's taken
Now, her smile was still there and she still said "Okay"

Although, this time it seemed just a bit more hard for her to say
Because, this time when she said it she knew that it wasn't sincere
For the first time since trying to find a seat in here
But, she proceeded
As she looked up she saw some folks leaving
Almost an entire row of people this was unbelievable
She moved quickly
Pulling her skirt down with every step
Trying to remain calm as she moved, trying to control her breath
A quick turn down the aisle…
Just a few more feet to go…
Just a few more steps to take…
Just a few more steps to make a few more and I'll be sitting
Just a few more feet she thought
A few more steps are all that's left to take as she continued to walk, but…
When she arrived… 3 jackets, 2 bags, 4 books and a brush is what she rushed over to see
That's what sat upon those chairs
Just another place she would leave
She hadn't noticed, but she had let out a sigh
It was an emotional sadness that was building up inside
She was a bit more nervous now than she was before
A bit more uncomfortable
But, still she was there
Now far off to the right she saw an empty seat
It was a lot further back than she would have wanted it to be
But, there it was no waiting, no occupancy
No signs of any kind of reserved seating
There was a gentleman who sat next to the empty seat she had her eyes on
Before long she had reached that empty seat she'd set her sights on
Upon arrival there a lady sat on the end of that row
Upon arrival she spoke, upon arrival she said "Hello"
She followed that up with "Excuse me" so that she could get by

But, this lady gave her no reply
She didn't move… she just sat there in that chair arms folded eyes forward not a word
As if she never even heard her speak
Even the expression on her face was bleak
But, for this girl all she saw was the seat
She kindly repeated herself thinking, perhaps she didn't hear me
Maybe I need to speak up, maybe I didn't speak clearly enough
So, she said "Excuse me" again
To which this lady replied, she who sat on the end
I heard you the first time! Go around! I aint movin'! Git here on time!
Whatever excitement she had at that moment was now gone
Whatever enthused attitude she once exuded was gone
What did returned to her instantly were those fears and insecurities
All of the pain she tried to hide, was now ten times magnified
She felt that shame return…
Shame for all of her past deeds for which she was ready to confess
Shame for which she'd managed to push deep down into her very debts
And all of those thoughts she fought so hard to ignore and resist
All had come rushing back to her mind quick
Her bottom lip began to quiver, but she smiled through it
And her hands began to sweat, but she smiled through it
And her legs began to shake, but she smiled through it
And her eyes began to water, but she smiled through it
And as the tears began to roll down her face…
And with that same smile still on her face…
She said to the lady softly "Okay"
Then she turned and slowly walked away
She headed down the church aisle until she reached the church corridors
Then she exited out the church doors… thanks to those privileged few
Those who were more concerned with saving and holding chairs
Rather than making room for a stranger so that they'd feel welcome there…
Those privileged few
Those who thought more of themselves and their comfort zone

Those who thought less of those in need or in search of a good church home
Those privileged few...
Those who are so use to their routine
So use to being in church, so use to doing their own thing
Those privileged few…
The crew…
Sitting amongst us clicked up
Reserving chairs so that those they know could sit there
She only came to get her heart fixed… her life changed
Well… maybe next time

WHO ARE YOU REALLY?

Are you a Christian? What side of the fence are you on? Do you practice what you preach? Are you the same no matter where you go or who you're with? Do people hate to see you come or love for you to stay? Are you a truth seeker? Are you a peace keeper or a hell raiser? Who are you, really?

I AM CHRISTIAN
Written by
Kevin K. King Sr.

What kind of a Christian are you?
Are you one who never pray, sometimes pray or always prays?
And when you do pray, is it just so folks can see you?
Or do you only pray when trouble forces you to?

What kind of Christian are you when visitors come to your church to worship with you?
Do you make them feel at home, what do you do?
Would you introduce yourself and maybe even offer them a seat?
Or do you sit there and not even speak?

What kind of Christian are you while services take place?
Are you rude, stubborn, don't want to move down to make space?
Do you chew gum more than you listen, perhaps talk more than you should?
Do you occasionally yell out GOD IS GOOD!?

What kind of a Christian are you when Christian folks aren't around, how do you get down then?
Are you still the good Christian?
Do you still fight the good fight the way the way a good Christian would fight?
Or do you easily get along with sin?

What kind of a Christian are you on the weekend?
Are you still the same Christian that started the week off to begin?
Or by now has this Christian stop being a Christian by weeks end only to start next week off being a Christian again?

What kind of Christian are you when bad weather is outside and you drive but, still won't make it out Sunday to church?
Are you the same Christian who drives when bad weather is outside but, you will make it out Monday to work?

What kind of a Christian are you when the pastors away?
Will you still come out and worship Sunday knowing that the pastor's away?
Or knowing this will you go out and kick hard that Saturday night because, you hadn't planned on being there Sunday no way, right?

What kind of a Christian are you after church, afterward?
What kind of a Christian are you after the choir after the pastor after the word?
What kind of a Christian are you after the music's been played after the song after the dance and praise?
What kind of Christian are the other six days?

What kind of a Christian are you at home, how you living?
Still holding that grudge against that family member not forgiving?
What kinds of examples are you setting for those who look up to you?
What's the attitude that you exude, what's your general mood?

What kind of a Christian are you at work?
Are you the same Christian at work who was just praising God a church?
Are you the same Christian who was just speaking in tongue praising God, now using that same tongue to cuss out folks on the job?

What kind of a Christian are you when the phone rings at one o'clock in the morning and you're at home...she's at home...you're alone...and she's alone...you're both grown...single and you say you're just friends?

What kind of Christian would you be then?

What kind of Christian are you when the rent or mortgage is due...when the phone bill is due...when the light, gas, water bills are due?
What words as a Christian would you then begin to shout?
When the pressure is on you what's gone come out?

MY NAME SAKE...

My son carries my name. I've been in his life since he sprang out of his mother in the delivery room. Early on we knew that he was special. Since he was a child he's always had a generous and compassionate heart to share and to give all that he's had to strangers, almost to a fault. He's without doubt, his mom's heart and joy, which in no way diminishes the love that she has for our other kids, but I believe in every family there's always that ONE who stands out and there was nothing she wouldn't do for him. He's always been easy to please, whatever you gave him he was happy to receive and he almost never fussed a lot about things he either had or didn't have. A super hyper child growing up a characteristic he no doubt picked up from me that drove his mom crazy, but she was on the job and could curve his active pace with a few simple authoritative commands which she did well. Kevin is the middle of our three kids and there's always something to be said about that middle child and there awkward position in the family, no longer the baby, but yet not the oldest. In many ways he's had to sacrifice more than his older sister and younger brother in the fact that he always had to share his things with his little brother and when it came to choosing first well, that honor went to his older sister. Without question we love our kids, but Kevin has always been special in his own way. But, such as life things change. People change. To my knowledge my son first starting getting into trouble at age fifteen, associating with gangs. After a while his grades dropped and he started breaking curfew hanging out smoking and drinking having sex. Soon thereafter the arrests came... loitering, trespassing, stealing, fighting and the lies, the lies were endless and the excuses were plenty. Things had gotten to such a bad place between my son and I that I had begun to dislike him. At first I thought it was hate that I felt towards my son, but it wasn't it was the other four letter word I felt... HURT. The pain I felt, the disappointment, the shame. I didn't understand what was happening with him. I didn't know who this person was nor did I seem to have a clue. But, it took my wife, thank God, who helped me to see this thing for what it was when she said to me it's not him, but the spirit inside of him that's trying to destroy his life. It was with those godly words of wisdom that I began to look upon my son with new eyes. Eyes of understanding even though I didn't like what I was still seeing my perception of him changed. So, for anyone who has a loved one that they've been struggling with in some form or another, don't give up on them... keep them lifted up in prayer. Put your trust in God. He's the one who designed and made them so who better to turn to than the source. I wrote this poem for my son to express all of the pain I was feeling, all of the disappointment, all of the anger, all of the hurt... I now know that it wasn't just for me to be encouraged, but for others who are going through this as well.

FAMILIAR STRANGER
Written by
Kevin K. King Sr.

The face seems familiar and I recognize the name
It's funny the more things stay the same they change
But, I know this face
Underneath all of the hardships of life the cuts and scars from fights, I recognize it
Through all of the crazy talk and weight loss, I recognize it
Through all of the foolishness the nonsense and the ignorance, I still recognize this face...
But, it's the spirit inside I hate
See, I know you but I don't
I wanna turn my back on you and leave you in your own private hell but, I can't...I won't
I wanna ignore you when I see you but, I can't so I don't
I wanna disown you but, I won't
I wanna toss you aside as if you were just some common trash but, I won't
See, you're not the one that I'm upset with
Yeah, it's you I have to talk to; it's you I have to address
But, you're just a conduit to this foolishness; you're just being used to play the role of a disrespectful, insensitive fool
And I'm upset behind all of this
The fact that he decided to pick you to attack, like I wasn't gone fight back
Like I was just gonna sit there and say nothing and let him do as he likes
I'm not gone let this stranger come in and just lay claim on your life
Despite the hell that he's been causing for me...causing for you
Despite the pain that he's been taking me through...taking us through
Because, when he picked you it wasn't just you that he's been trying to destroy

But, the potential placed in you God wants to deploy
Trying to destroy me through you...hurt me too
Get me to give up on you because, that's what he'll like for me to do
Give up, throw in the towel
Wish you well somehow
Leave you alone and watch you die
Discourage me not to try but, it's all a lie
And I'll cry if I have to cry
I'll share tears if I have to because I don't understand why
I'll even fight you if I have to because you mean just that much
Refuse to lose you to this nonsense, I refuse to give up and throw my hands up in frustration and quit
Even though it hurts me to the core, the very pit of my stomach
And if I have to feed that nonsense it's gone starve to death
And when I feel like I aint got nothing left...
I'll call a few saints up and ask them to pray
And we'll all flood heaven with prayer request that day
And then we'll follow that up with praise as we consider it done, call it a rap
Because, I'm taking your life back
Yeah, the face seems familiar...and I recognize the name
It's funny...the more things stay the same, they change
But, I know you...and I love you...and I'm not giving up on you
I love you, son

THIS IS MY OFFICIAL INTRO...

This is a constant reminder to ME about my purpose with this, one of the many gifts, God has entrusted me with. It's a self-check a self-examination about WHO I am and WHOSE'S I am and that it's not about pleasing man, but GOD first and foremost. This is EXACTLY what I said it is a reminder to <u>ME</u>. Period! That's it, that's all.

REMINDER TO SELF
Written by
Kevin K. King Sr.

For do I now persuade men, or God? Or do I seek to please men? For if I yet pleased men, I should not be the servant of Christ.

Galatians chpt.1 vrs.10

The minute I start doing this to please you I'm through
The minute I start doing this just for the applause I hope God cancels it all
It's not about entertaining you
And while I do understand the entertainment in what I do, I'm simply saying it is not my priority…you can get anyone for that
You can get anyone to stand before you and display lyrical word play that will amaze and astonish you… anyone to amuse you
And God bless'em
My goal is to give you something of substance, to pour something of value into you
Other wise, what's the point in what I do
This is a reminder to self or rather this is my-self check
I not tryin' to impress you
That's not what I'm suppose to do
Hope that you accept me or even co-sign my ability
Because, in the end I'm not looking for your approval or for you to validate me
There's only one who I'm trying to please G.O.D
This is a reminder to self or rather this is my-self check
I'm not trying to keep up with folks
I can't flip the script, go spiritual then hit you with the erotic
I've got to be who I say I be
For me I've got to have standards
I've got to have who I say I am character
I ain't trying to compete with nobody
I ain't concerned about status, I ain't concerned with whether or not I have it or who knows me or who likes me or what's my popularity
I ain't tryin' to fit in with the Jones
Never felt this need to fit in or belong with… anyone or anything
This is a reminder to my-self
That I can't get caught up in self
Yeah, it's okay to have confidence

But, I can't afford to forget where my gifts come from
I can't afford to be that dumb
I can't afford to pat myself on the back for a job well done
I've got to learn to hold my tongue at times, sit down and shut up
Because it ain't about the shine or the rush to be seen…
Been there done that, besides…
If I gotta brag about how cold I am it's really more of a lie than a fact… and the fact of the matter is this
I not concerned with name recognition… titles or positions means nothin'
But, is what I'm saying worth somethin' is the question
If not, I have failed you
Not that you have failed to get it
But, it was how my presentation was presented
It's what I stood here and represented
So I ask the questions
What am I up here for? What am I doing? What have I done? Who have I encouraged of helped?
Or am I just in this for self?
Who have I inspired? Who have I made an impact on?
Because, if I'm just up here for the attention them my intentions are wrong
This is a reminder to self…
This ain't a knock on no one else just a reminder to self to keep self in check because self can be selfish
Self-centered can self be, self-serving…
Believing it's deserving of all the praise
All of the accolades
I find myself having to check myself when I write…
I found myself trying to change what I write to fit what you'll like
And when that happens I put the pen down and stop
And if I've gone too far God hits with writer's block
This reminder is to remind me that this ain't about me
That it ain't about saying what's popular so that folks would like me
It's to remind me that GOD has assigned me to help
This is a reminder to my-self not to forget or better yet… this is my-self check

THROUGH THE TEST AND TRIALS

For all of the things that my wife had to endure... a poem
is the least of which I can do for her... (K.A.B)

FOR, B.J.
Written by
Kevin K. King Sr.

Now, outside of God the greatest inspiration in my life is my wife
She embodies the very essence of the term strong, intelligent,
beautiful, black woman
This recognition of mine for you is long, long overdue
See, you've put up with more from me throughout the years than you
had to so, I owe you... everything
Everything I have to give to you and more
I need to put my check in your hands soon as I walk through the door
Sounds absurd? No, it's what you deserve
See, you deserve to pick that house out that you want, I want to get it
Bills that need to be paid, don't worry about it, I've got it
I want to make your life style as comfortable in every way
I want to one day be in the position to leave you with the option of
working one more day
I want to send you off shopping and when you think you've spent too
much
I want to assure that when you come home with bags in hand that, you
haven't spent enough
All those folks from our past that didn't think we'd last...
Those folks who plotted on us from the start, to try and tear us apart
But, thank God who spoke to my heart and told me...
No matter what, this one here, she's for you
I designed it that way and I don't make mistakes
I put this woman here to be your help-mate
Painful circumstances I allowed to last longer
I put those things in places so together you'd be stronger... and you are

That's why I need to treat you the way God treats his church and do all I can for you

Because you're worth it

That's why I can honestly speak on the things that we've been through

That's why I can openly and publicly say to you I love you... because, I do... indeed I do

Spending my life with you through the hardest of times...

You've made it easier on my mind

You've provided me with a level of comfort only a good woman can

It's not about standing by your man but, helping your man to stand

So, I'm motivated to succeed

Motivated to achieve and having you in my life is just what I need because, you believe in me

Now, outside of God, who I put first

The greatest inspiration in my life was then and is now... my wife

I'M NOT LETTING GO...

No temptation has seized you except what is common to man. And God is faithful; he will not let you be tempted beyond what you can bear. But when you are tempted, he will also provide a way out so that you can stand up under it.

1

Corinthians 10:13 (NIV)

STAYING UNDER
Written by
Kevin K. King Sr.

I aint movin'... I aint goin' nowhere... I'm stayin' here... I'm stayin' put
And I don't care how it looks...I'm goin' through this
I aint leavin'... and I aint runnin'... and I aint turnin' 'round drawin' back
I've come too far for that
And it's been hard
And I've probably frowned more than I've smiled
And it gets hard to believe and have faith after a while because of the pain...
The frustrations... feelings of loneliness
Still... I just can't quit
And I want to
I wanna give up and give in
I wanna go back to that life I was livin' where I was livin' with sin
Where bad habits were too hard to break
And it seemed your word was even harder for me to embrace
I wanna go back to that place... it felt safe
I wanna give in to all those sins again... just to escape
I wanna give up and stop trying because of the pain that I feel...
I just want it to stop...

But, never the less, your will
And it hurts...
It hurts in my heart...
It hurts me to stay...
Hurts me when I lay down to go to sleep at night...
Hurts when I wake...
Hurts everyday...
And in my private time... it even hurts when I pray
Because, I start to feel that you don't love me... or even care
what I say
But, I aint movin'
And I have days filled with doubt
I have days where I'm afraid to say or claim I'm coming out...
because I don't believe it
It's hard to...
It's hard for me to do...
It's hard for me to believe when all I feel is the hell I'm going
through
I've been in this place for so long that when good news comes
along I cancel it out
I'm afraid to let joy come out my mouth because, when I do...
I believe more trouble's coming too
So, it's hard to praise you in the mist of the storm I'm going
through
But, I ai't movin'
And the agony in my heart don't let up, it don't seem to subside
And when it does I'm in too much grief to recognize that it has
Comes from feeling bad for a long time

Comes from having to fight just to keep faith from leavin' my mind
But, I'm tryin' and I keep tryin'
But, for all of my efforts I have set backs and so I keep cryin'
I keep fallin' but, I keep risin'
But, I keep fallin' but, I keep tryin'
But, I aint movin'
Seems the more I pray the harder things gets
Seems my troubles only multiply from one day to the next
I can't seem to get it right...
I try but, it's like I'm not trying enough
So, I get discouraged... and I just wanna give up
But, I aint movin'
I keep goin'... I keep diggin'... I keep grindin'...
I keep pressin'... I keep pushin'... I keep fightin'...
I've got my arms stretched out to you, Lord I'm reachin'...I'm tryin'
I'm tryin' to hold on, God... but, I'm tired
I'm tired of the pain
I'm tired of the emotional turmoil!
I'm tired the emotional strain!
I'm tired of havin' to fake how I feel when the pain is real!
I'm tired of folks only offering me words of scriptures to deal... with my pain
I'm not negating the word... right now it's just hard to receive
I need someone who can also relate to me in my valley
I need someone who can come down my street... and talk to me
So, I aint movin'

Even though it hurts...
Even though I'm in pain and I'm exhausted and I don't wanna
go through this
Even though I get frustrated and my spirit gets depressed
I'm aint leaving from this place, Lord not until I've been
blessed... by you
I'm goin' through this, however long it takes...
And I don't care about any kind of trouble that I face!
I'm goin' through this because I'm tired of turnin' around goin'
back to the same mess ...
That has been keepin' me locked in the same nonsense
I'm goin' through this... come hell or high water
And since I've been goin' through hell then I can use some fresh
water
Because, I'm tired of back slidin', I'm tired lyin' to myself
I pray for guidance but, then I turn away from your help...
I'm goin' through this... whatever it takes, whatever the case
Whatever obstacle's that try to rise up and stand in my way
Whatever the problem! Whatever the issues are I don't care!
I aint leavin' like I came in here! I AIN'T GOIN' NOWHERE!
I'm willing to go through what I've got to, to get to where I
need to get to in you...
So I can do what you've called me to do
BECAUSE I AIN'T MOVIN'!
Not until I've been made new!
And if this is the process that I have to go through...
If you've got to bless me to break me all over again!
If that's the process then let's just let the healing begin!
And if cryin' is part of the process, then let me cry

If pain is part of my growth help me rise
Leave that wound on the outside, leave that scar where it is
Even if you take away those things in my life I hold dear
If it servers YOUR purpose... then don't leave me out
Have your way so that others can see what your glory's about
Because, I've made up my mind...
No matter what...
I aint movin'...
I ain't goin' nowhere...
I'm stayin' right here...
I'm stayin' put...
I really don't care anymore about it looks...
I don't...
I'm committed to this...
I won't quit...
I'm determined...
I'm... staying... under

Made in the USA
Charleston, SC
28 July 2013